BlackBerry Pearl For Dummies®

Cheat Sheet

Calendar Application Shortcuts

The following shortcuts work in Day, Week, and Month views:

! Q W	Return to today's date in your current Calendar view	**6 J K** Go to the next day in your current Calendar view
4 D F	Go to the previous day in your current Calendar view	

Day view

These shortcuts work in Day view, with the Quick Entry option disabled:

0 + SPACE	Go to the next day	
scroll trackball horizontally	Go to the next or previous day	
5 G H	Look into an existing appointment (or if no appointment exists, open a new appointment screen)	
! Q W	Jump to today's date in Day view	
2 T Y	Move up by the hour	
3 U I	Move down by the hour	

Week view

These shortcuts work in Week view:

9 M	Go to next week
3 U I	Go to previous week
5 G H	Look into an existing appointment (or if no appointment exists, open a new appointment screen)
scroll trackball vertically	Move up or down by the hour
scroll trackball horizontally	Move between days
! Q W	Jump to today's date in Week view
· ◀)) O P	Make a new appointment

Month view

These shortcuts work in Month view:

horizontally scroll trackball	Move horizontally across the month
vertically scroll trackball	Move vertically across the month
9 M	Go to the next month
3 U I	Go to the previous month
· ◀)) O P	Make a new appointment
5 G H	Look at an existing appointment (or if no appointment exists, open a new appointment screen)

For Dummies: Bestselling Book Series for Beginners

BlackBerry Pearl For Dummies®

Cheat Sheet

Message Application Shortcuts while in the Message List

Sort/Filter

List incoming e-mail only	ALT+ **3 UI**	List SMS messages only	ALT+ **? AS**	
List phone calls only	ALT+ **· ◄)) OP**	List voice mail only	ALT+ **7 CV**	

Navigating

Oldest e-mail	**7 CV**	Read next unread e-mail	*** SYM**	Move up in e-mail list	**2 TY**
Newest e-mail	**1 ER**	Next page	**9 M**	Move down in e-mail list	**3 UI**
Previous day	**4 DF**		**0 + SPACE**	Open e-mail	**5 GH**
Next day	**6 JK**	Previous page	**3 UI**		or press trackball

Other shortcuts

Compose e-mail	**' L**	Reply to	**! QW**	Reply to and include yourself	**? AS**
Forward e-mail	**· ◄)) OP**				

Message Application Shortcuts while in an E-mail

Top of page	**1 ER**	Previous page	**3 UI**	Previous line	**2 TY**
Bottom of page	**7 CV**	Next e-mail	**6 JK**	Next line	**3 UI**
Next page	**9 M**	Previous e-mail	**4 DF**	Read next unread e-mail	*** SYM**
	0 + SPACE	Forward e-mail	**· ◄)) OP**		

Wiley, the Wiley Publishing logo, For Dummies, the Dummies Man logo, the For Dummies Bestselling Book Series logo and all related trade dress are trademarks or registered trademarks of John Wiley & Sons, Inc. and/or its affiliates. All other trademarks are property of their respective owners.

For Dummies: Bestselling Book Series for Beginners

BlackBerry® Pearl™ FOR DUMMIES®

by Robert Kao & Marie-Claude Kao

Dante Sarigumba & Yosma Sarigumba

Wiley Publishing, Inc.

BlackBerry® Pearl™ For Dummies®
Published by
Wiley Publishing, Inc.
111 River Street
Hoboken, NJ 07030-5774

www.wiley.com

WILEY

About the Authors

Robert Kao is one well-rounded professional. His ability to translate his technical knowledge and communicate in many languages with users of all types inevitably led him to develop BlackBerry applications for various financial firms in New York City — that truly global city. A graduate of Columbia University — with a Computer Engineering degree, of course — he currently lives in Somerset, New Jersey.

Dante Sarigumba is a long time user of BlackBerry, a gizmo enthusiast, and the coauthor of *BlackBerry For Dummies*. He is a co-host of the Mobile Computing Authority biweekly podcast. As a Software Developer, he works for a major investment bank in New York and lives in South Brunswick, New Jersey with his wife Rosemarie and two sons, Dean and Drew.

Marie-Claude Kao graduated with a degree in French to English translation from the University of Ottawa. She and her husband, Robert, have been long-time BlackBerry enthusiasts. In the past, Marie-Claude has worked for the Canadian government as a technical translator and currently works in New Brunswick, New Jersey.

Yosma Sarigumba is a full-time consultant specializing in distributed applications and Web application development. She also loves to play with the latest tech gadgets. She utilizes her BlackBerry Pearl extensively to keep life with her two active sons as smooth sailing as possible.

Authors' Acknowledgments

I would like to thank my father (MHK) and mother (SYT) for everything they've done for me, because I wouldn't be here without their kindness and support. Long overdue thanks to Prof. Kathy Eden of Columbia University for her patience and guidance and for putting up with an engineer in her literature class.

—Robert Kao

Thanks to my mother (Isabel) for everything and thanks to my aunt (Fabiana) for treating me like a son. Thank you for your support and encouragement. Also, thanks to Dean and Drew for being such wonderful kids.

—Dante Sarigumba

I would like to thank my parents Manon and Daniel, my sisters Geneviève and Fanny, my husband Rob, and my daughter Jade for their unconditional love and support. Special thanks to the "Translation Babes" in Canada for their friendship.

—Marie-Claude Kao

Special thanks to my family: Dan, Dean, and Drew, to my parents, Jun and Bong Orbon, to my sister Weng and the entire Mirasol clan for being there for me every time I hatch yet another hare-brained scheme. Their love and support have gotten me through some really rough spots. Each and every day I thank God for every minute that I spend with all of you.

—Yosma Sarigumba

Collectively, we'd like to thank Greg Croy, Carol McClendon, and Wiley Publishing for kicking off this book. Thanks as well to Richard Evers of Research In Motion for a wealth of information and guidance. We would also like to thank Susan Pink for working through this book swiftly with diligence. Without all of you, this book would not have been possible.

—Rob and Marie-Claude & Dante and Yosma

Publisher's Acknowledgments

We're proud of this book; please send us your comments through our online registration form located at www.dummies.com/register/.

Some of the people who helped bring this book to market include the following:

Acquisitions, Editorial, and Media Development

Project Editor: Susan Pink

Acquisitions Editor: Greg Croy

Technical Editor: Richard Evers

Editorial Manager: Jodi Jensen

Media Development Specialists: Angela Denny, Kate Jenkins, Steven Kudirka, Kit Malone

Media Development Coordinator: Laura Atkinson

Media Project Supervisor: Laura Moss

Media Development Manager: Laura VanWinkle

Media Development Associate Producer: Richard Graves

Editorial Assistant: Amanda Foxworth

Sr. Editorial Assistant: Cherie Case

Cartoons: Rich Tennant (www.the5thwave.com)

Composition Services

Project Coordinator: Heather Kolter

Layout and Graphics: Carl Byers, Joyce Haughey, Stephanie D. Jumper, Laura Pence

Proofreaders: Laura Albert, Charles Spencer, Lisa Stiers

Indexer: Techbooks

Anniversary Logo Design: Richard J. Pacifico

Publishing and Editorial for Technology Dummies

Richard Swadley, Vice President and Executive Group Publisher

Andy Cummings, Vice President and Publisher

Mary Bednarek, Executive Acquisitions Director

Mary C. Corder, Editorial Director

Publishing for Consumer Dummies

Diane Graves Steele, Vice President and Publisher

Joyce Pepple, Acquisitions Director

Composition Services

Gerry Fahey, Vice President of Production Services

Debbie Stailey, Director of Composition Services

Contents at a Glance

Table of Contents

Introduction

*H*i there, and welcome to *BlackBerry Pearl For Dummies.* Having purchased a BlackBerry Pearl, this is a great book to have around if you want to discover new features or you need something to slap open and use as a quick reference. If you don't have a BlackBerry Pearl yet (but plan to get one) and have some basic questions (such as "What is a BlackBerry Pearl?" or "How can a Pearl help me be more productive?"), you can benefit by reading this book cover to cover. Regardless of your current BlackBerry User Status — BUS, for short — we're here to help you get the most out of your BlackBerry.

We can tell you, right off the bat, that a BlackBerry Pearl is not a fruit you find at the supermarket nor a jewel. Rather, it is an always-connected handheld device that has e-mail capabilities with a built-in Internet browser and the latest in convergent smart phones with advanced media features and a camera. With your BlackBerry, you are in the privileged position of always being able to receive e-mail, browse the Web, and have fun listening to music and taking pictures.

On top of that, a BlackBerry has all the features you'd expect from a personal organizer, including a calendar, to-do lists, and memos. Oh, and did we mention that a BlackBerry also has a mobile phone built in? Talk about multitasking! Imagine being stuck on a commuter train: With your BlackBerry by your side, you can compose e-mail while conducting a conference call — all from the comfort of your seat.

In this book, we show you all the basics but then go the extra mile by highlighting some of the lesser-known (but still handy) features of the Pearl. Your Pearl can work hard for you when you need it as well as play hard when you want it to.

About This Book

BlackBerry Pearl For Dummies is written to be a comprehensive user guide as well as a quick user reference. This book is designed so that you certainly can read it cover to cover if you want, but you don't need to. Feel free to jump around while you explore the different functionalities of your BlackBerry. We cover basic and advanced topics, but we stick to those that we consider the most practical and frequently used. Also, we provide ample screen images so that you can relate to the topics even when you're not holding your BlackBerry Pearl. Screen images used throughout the book are based on the T-Mobile Zen theme and may vary if you are not using this theme.

Who Are You?

In writing this book, we tried to be considerate of your needs, but because we've never met you, our image of you is as follows. If you find that some of these images are true about you, this might just be the book for you:

- ✔ You have a BlackBerry Pearl, and you want to find out how to get the most from it. Or you don't have a BlackBerry Pearl yet, and you're wondering what one could do for you.

- ✔ You want to take advantage of the many fun features of your BlackBerry Pearl, including taking pictures, listening to music, and watching video clips.

- ✔ You're looking for a book that doesn't assume you know all the jargon and tech terms used in the PDA industry. (PDA stands for personal digital assistant, by the way.) Take that, you jargon, you!

- ✔ You want a reference that shows you, step by step, how to do useful and cool things with a BlackBerry without bogging you down with unnecessary background or theory.

- ✔ You're tired of hauling your ten-pound laptop with you on trips, and you're wondering how to turn your BlackBerry into a miniature traveling office.

- ✔ You no longer want to be tied to your desktop system for the critical activities in your life, such as sending and receiving e-mail, checking your calendar for appointments, and surfing the Web.

What's in This Book

BlackBerry Pearl For Dummies consists of five parts, and each part consists of chapters related to that part's theme.

Part I: Meet and Greet Your BlackBerry Pearl

Part I starts with the basics of your BlackBerry Pearl. You know: What it is, what you can do with it, and what the parts are. We also show you how to personalize and express yourself through your BlackBerry. This part wraps up with must-knows about security and where to go for help when you get into trouble with your BlackBerry.

Part II: Getting Organized with Your Pearl

Part II deals with the fact that your BlackBerry is also a full-fledged PDA. We show you how to get your BlackBerry to keep your contacts in its Address Book as well as how to manage your appointments and meetings in Calendar. We also show you how to take some notes and safely keep your passwords. As you'll see, most BlackBerry applications interconnect, working hard for you.

Part III: Getting Multimedia and Online with Your Pearl

Part III shows you how you can use the true strengths of the BlackBerry — its always-connected e-mail and its Web surfing functionality — but it doesn't stop there. We also point out how you can use other forms of messages on the BlackBerry that you might not have known about, such as PIN-to-PIN messages, BlackBerry Messenger, and Instant Messaging from the popular IM networks. We feature the ability of your BlackBerry Pearl to capture cool pictures and, to top it off, satisfy your senses by playing media files such as music and video clips.

Part IV: Working with Desktop Manager

In Part IV, we detail the BlackBerry Desktop Manager and show you some of the hoops you can put it through with your Pearl, including making backups. And we didn't forget to cover important stuff such as data-syncing your appointments and contacts with desktop applications such as Outlook.

Part V: The Part of Tens

All *For Dummies* books include The Part of Tens at the end, and this book is no different. In Part V, we show you where to get cool BlackBerry accessories and download useful applications.

Icons in This Book

 This book rarely delves into the geeky, technical details, but when it does, this icon warns you. Read on if you want to get under the hood a little, or just skip ahead if you aren't interested in the gory details.

 Here's where you can find not-so-obvious tricks that can make you a BlackBerry power user in no time. Pay special attention to the paragraphs with this icon to get the most out of your BlackBerry.

 Look out! This icon tells you how to avoid trouble before it starts.

 This icon highlights an important point that you don't want to forget because it just might come up again. We'd never be so cruel as to spring a pop quiz on you, but paying attention to these details can definitely help you.

Where to Go from Here

If you want to find out more about the book or have a question or comment for the authors, please visit us at

```
www.dummies.com/go/blackberrypearl
```

Now you can dive in! Give Chapter 1 a quick look to get an idea of where this book takes you, and then feel free to head straight to your chapter of choice.

Part I
Meet and Greet Your BlackBerry Pearl

The 5th Wave   By Rich Tennant

"Hold on, Barbara. Let me visit AnimalPlanet.com to see if they have a troubleshooting guide for this."

In this part . . .

The road to a happy and collaborative relationship with your BlackBerry Pearl starts here. Chapter 1 covers all the nuts and bolts — how things work, the Pearl's look and feel, and connectivity. Chapter 2 discusses how you can navigate with ease to the world of BlackBerry Pearl, offering timesaving shortcuts. Finally, Chapter 3 shows you how to customize Pearl and make it your own.

Chapter 1

Your BlackBerry Is Not an Edible Fruit

*B*ecause you're reading this book, you probably have a BlackBerry Pearl (um, and we're pretty sure that you're not eating it). We're just curious, though — what convinced you to buy this particular handheld mobile device? Was it the always-connected e-mail? Or the 1.3 mega-pixel camera? Or the microSD slot capability? Or was it the really good sales pitch? We know; the list could go on and on — and we might never hit on the exact reason why you got yours. For whatever reason you bought your BlackBerry Pearl, congratulations; you made an intelligent choice.

The same smarts that made you buy your Pearl are clearly at it again. This time, your native intelligence led you to pick up this book, perhaps because your intuition is telling you that there's more to this whole BlackBerry than meets the eye.

Your hunch is right. Your BlackBerry *can* help you do more things than you could ever think of. For example, your BlackBerry is a whiz at making phone calls, but it's also a computer that you can use to check your e-mail as well as surf the Web. We're talking *World Wide* Web here, so the sky's the limit. Help is always at your fingertips rather than sitting on some desk at home or at the office. Need to check out the reviews of that restaurant on the corner? Need to see (right now) what's showing in your local movie theaters, or what the weather will be like later tonight, or the best place to shop? Need to get directions to that cozy bed and breakfast, or news headlines, or stock quotes? Want to do some online chatting or view some pictures online and download them? You can do all these things (and more) by using your BlackBerry.

 BlackBerry Pearl is also a full-fledged personal digital assistant (PDA). Out of the box, it provides you with the organizational tools you need to set up to-do lists, manage your appointments, take care of your address books, and more.

Being armed with a device that's a sleek phone, a camera, a portal flash drive, an Internet connection, and a PDA all built into one makes you a power person. With your BlackBerry (along with this resourceful book), you really can improve your productivity, better organize yourself, and increase your cool factor. Watch out, world! Person bearing a BlackBerry Pearl coming through!

If you stick with us throughout this book, you'll find out all you need to get the most out of your device or maybe even stave off (or save) a troubled relationship. (Well, the last one is a bit of an exaggeration, but we got your attention, right?)

Knowing Your BlackBerry History

Your BlackBerry Pearl is truly a wondrous device, boasting many features beyond your ordinary mobile phone. And its "sudden" popularity didn't happen overnight. Like any other good product out there, BlackBerry Pearl has come a long way from its (relatively humble) beginnings.

In the days when the Palm Pilot ruled the PDA world, Research in Motion (RIM, the maker of the BlackBerry) was busy in its lab, ignoring the then-popular graffiti input method to design its own device with the QWERTY keyboard — the kind of keyboard people were already used to from working on their PCs. RIM didn't stop there, however. It also added an always-connected e-mail capability, making this device a must-have among government officials as well as professionals in the finance and health industries.

To meet the needs of government officials and industry professionals, RIM made reliability, security, and durability the priorities when manufacturing its devices. Today, the BlackBerry Pearl comes from the same line of RIM family products, inheriting all the good genes while boosting usability and especially multimedia capabilities. As a result, BlackBerry Pearl has become the hippest smart-phone — and no longer just for big corporate hot-shots and government officials.

How It Works: The Schematic Approach

For those of you who always ask, "How do they do that?" you don't have to go far; this little section is just for you.

The role of the network service provider

Along with wondering how your BlackBerry actually works, you might also be wondering why you didn't get your BlackBerry from RIM instead of a network service provider such as Cingular or T-Mobile? Why did you need to go through a middle-person? After all, RIM makes BlackBerry.

Those are excellent questions — and here's a quick-and-dirty answer. RIM needs a delivery system — a communication medium, as it were — for its technology to work. Not in a position to come up with such a delivery system all by its lonesome, RIM partnered (and built alliances across the globe) with what developed into its network service providers — the usual suspects (meaning the big cellphone companies).

These middle-providers support the wireless network for your BlackBerry so that you have signals to connect to the BlackBerry Internet Service — which means you can get all those wonderful e-mails (and waste so much valuable time surfing the Internet). See Figure 1-1 for a schematic overview of this process.

Network service providers don't build alliances for nothing, right? In return, RIM gave them the right to brand their names on the BlackBerry they offer for sale. For example, a T-Mobile Pearl may look different from a similar model you would get from Vodafone. Which leads to another question: Do BlackBerry functionalities differ from phone model to phone model? Quick answer: In the core BlackBerry applications (such as Tasks and Address Book), you find no major differences. However, some BlackBerry features, such as Instant Messaging, might or might not be supported by the network service provider. (See Chapter 8 for more details on Instant Messaging.)

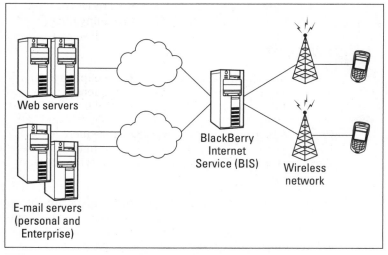

Figure 1-1: Your e-mail travels to your BlackBerry via service providers.

Connecting to your personal computer

Nowadays, a personal computer is a household necessity. We spend so much time on them, and so much information is stored in them. It should come as no surprise that BlackBerry works hand-in-hand with your PC. The USB cable that comes with your BlackBerry does more than just charge your device. All the chapters in Part IV are dedicated to guiding you in making use of this important connection with the help of the BlackBerry Desktop Manager and all the utilities that come with it. You find discussions in Chapter 13 on how to sync your device with the Personal Information Manager data that you keep in your PC. Chapter 14 guides you on how to back up almost anything in your BlackBerry, down to your desktop. Lastly, Chapter 15 shows you how to use the Pearl and its microSD slot as storage that goes where you go.

Doing the BlackBerry world-traveler thing

If you purchased your Pearl from T-Mobile or Cingular, chances are that your BlackBerry Pearl will continue to work when you travel to, say, London or Beijing. All you need to worry about is turning on your Pearl (and maybe the extra roaming charges). Because your BlackBerry Pearl is quad band, it will work in more than 90 different countries.

What is quad band? Basically, different cellphone networks in different countries operate in different frequencies. For example, the United States operates two frequencies: 850 and 1900 MHz; Canada, 850 and 1900 MHz; Europe and Asia Pacific, 900 and 1800 MHz. Your Pearl is designed to work in these four frequencies — 850/900/ 1800/1900 MHz — so you are covered no matter where you go. Well, almost. Check with your network service provider before you hop on a plane just to be sure.

Two dominant technologies compete in the worldwide cellphone industry today:

- **Code Division Multiple Access (CDMA):** This is available in the United States through Verizon Wireless.

- **Global System for Mobile Communication (GSM):** This is a tad older than its CDMA rival. This is available in the United States through Cingular and T-Mobile.

Nothing stands still in this world, and this saying is proven by the fact that GSM has spawned *Global Packet Radio Service* (GPRS) and EDGE, a second-generation technology that has been growing in popularity because it works on the same GSM phone infrastructure. This combo GSM/GPRS is also available in the United States through most of the major network service providers. As you might have guessed, GSM/GPRS competes in the marketplace against CDMA.

Why is this a factor? Or, to put this more bluntly, what's it to you? Well, because CDMA and GSM/GPRS aren't compatible — which is what happens when you have competing technologies going for all the marbles in the marketplace — your phone works on only one technology. When you travel outside North America, you face the burning question: "CDMA or GSM/GPRS?" (The non-acronym version of this question is, "Will my BlackBerry work on this country's network or won't it?") If you currently work with GSM/GPRS, you should be okay because most non-North American countries are on GSM/GPRS networks. If you're a CDMA kind of person, you might have some "issues," as they say. When in doubt, talk to your network service provider.

Oh, the Things You Can Do!

Unlike the traditional BlackBerry, your Pearl is a work of art when it comes to smart phones. But besides its looks, the always-connected e-mail is likely first in the long list of reasons why you got your Pearl in the first place. And, if you need to go global, you can use your BlackBerry in 90+ countries. Just hop off your flight, turn on your Pearl, and voilà! e-mails on your Pearl while you're 6000 miles away from home. See the earlier "Doing the BlackBerry world-traveler thing" section for more info.) Generally speaking, you can receive and send e-mails just like when you're at home.

Although e-mail is Pearl's strength, that's not the only thing it can do. This section goes beyond e-mail to point out some of the other major benefits you can get from your device.

All-in-one multimedia center

Before the BlackBerry Pearl arrived on the scene, many consumers were hesitant about purchasing a BlackBerry due to the lack of multimedia functions such as a camera and audio playback. The Pearl changed all that, with more features than a typical consumer might expect. Not only does the Pearl have a high-resolution, 1.3 mega-pixel camera (see Chapter 11), but it also has a memory slot for a microSD chip (see Chapter 15). That means your Pearl can function as an mp3 player, a portal video player, a portable flash drive, and your personal photo collection (see Chapter 11). It's like having an iPod and then some. Can your iPod do the following?

Internet at your fingertips

Yup, you can browse the Web with your Pearl. Even better, you can continue chatting with your friends through Instant Messenger, just as though you never left your desktop computer (see Chapter 8). You can also get up-to-the-minute information when you want it, when you need it. Imagine getting an alert when your stock is tanking. True, that's not a good thing to happen, but this information is critical if you want to act in a timely manner.

If you're not into stocks, how about getting sports and weather information? Or maybe traffic alerts? Say you want to know the best restaurants in town for that special evening — birthday, anniversary, first date. Many services that are available on the Internet are available to you also on your Pearl.

With the growing popularity of the device, software developers outside RIM are taking advantage of this growing market — which means literally hundreds of applications are now out there for you to download.

Download? Absolutely! BlackBerry supports the downloading of applications and games through the BlackBerry Browser. And of course, it's wireless. For example, you can download more productivity tools such as spreadsheet applications or an exciting game of Texas-Hold 'em. The number of BlackBerry applications and games is growing — and growing fast.

To be honest, there's no way to foresee how many applications will be on the market when this book is published. And the price of an application varies, depending on how sophisticated the program is, so we can't give firm numbers. But if you're curious, check out Part V, where we describe some of the best applications and games out there.

Intrigued? Your questions about how your Pearl can take advantage of the Web and wireless download are answered in due time (in Chapter 9, to be precise).

Me and my great personal assistant

You might be saying, "But I'm really a busy person, and I don't have time to browse the Web. What I *do* need is an assistant to help me better organize my day-to-day tasks." If you can afford one, by all means go ahead and hire a personal assistant. If not, the next best thing is a personal *digital* assistant (PDA). Many PDAs are on the market today; the most popular ones are marketed by Palm and WinCE. Getting a PDA can be a big help — and much less expensive than hiring a secretary.

So, are we telling you to go out and buy a PDA? No way! Put away that credit card because you don't need to go that route.

Whip out your Pearl and take a closer look. That's right, your Pearl is also a full-fledged PDA, able to help you remember all your acquaintances (see Chapter 4), manage your appointments (Chapter 5), keep a to-do list (Chapter 6), and much more.

Me and my chatty self

With all the features just described above, your Pearl is also a full-featured phone. With voice dialing, and the ability to carry out conference calls with you as the moderator, your Pearl isn't like other cellphones out there. To learn more about your Pearl Phone, see Chapter 10.

Look, Dad, no hands!

Your BlackBerry comes equipped with an earphone that doubles as a mike for hands-free talking. This accessory is your doctor's prescription for preventing the stiff neck that comes from wedging your BlackBerry with your shoulder against your ear. At the very minimum, it helps free your hands so you can eat Chinese takeout. And, if you happen to be a New York resident, you're required by law to use an earphone while driving when you use a cellphone. (Not that we recommend using your cellphone while driving, but if you really need to make that call, going hands-free is better and safer.)

But RIM didn't stop with just your standard (wired) earphones. BlackBerry also supports cool, new wireless earphones/mikes — the ones based on Bluetooth technology. "But how could a bizarrely colored tooth help me here?" you might ask. Fooled you! *Bluetooth* is a codename for a (very) short-distance wireless technology first used to connect simple devices such as computer accessories, but that is now becoming more common on cellphones, specifically on wireless earphones/mikes.

Final BlackBerry Tidbits

The main concerns most of us have when buying a product are quality and reliability. Will the product last? Will it perform as the flier says? Will I regret having bought this item six months down the road? This section looks at some of the hardware features that make buying the BlackBerry Pearl a wise purchase.

Power efficiency

Now, anyone who has had an ear to the ground regarding BlackBerry knows its reputation as a highly efficient little machine when it comes to power consumption. Even with the addition of colored and high-resolution screens, the power consumption of the Pearl still has a 15-day standby time and close to 4 hours talk time. So, when the salesperson offers you a special deal on a second battery, simply tell him or her that you'll think about it. With the Pearl's standard battery, you'll have more than enough power.

Memory management

When you first receive your BlackBerry Pearl, the device definitely has ample free memory. However, that memory — which is used for applications that come with your Pearl and for other applications you download — does not grow as you use BlackBerry. You're stuck with a fixed amount of memory, which can prove limiting over time. As you install more and more applications, this free memory gets used up. In fact, you could eventually run out of memory altogether.

Don't confuse this fixed amount of memory with the memory available through the microSD slot. A microSD chip can store mp3s, portable videos and pictures that you download or load from your PC.

Does your device die when you run out of memory? No, thank goodness. Your BlackBerry is capable of monitoring the free memory on your device. If you're ever in danger of reaching your upper limits, the BlackBerry has a memory management tool that cleans house to free this limited resource.

BlackBerry applications right out of the box are capable of figuring out what data isn't that important. For example, the BlackBerry Browser caches data to enhance your experience when browsing the Web. *Caches* use local copies of Web pages to speed up the reloading of previously visited Web sites, so they are generally good things to have around. However, this cache also takes up space. When the OS tells Browser that the device is reaching its upper memory limit and that it needs to do some house cleaning, Browser deletes this cache. This is also true for Message, which deletes e-mails you've already read, starting from the oldest and working its way backward.

Curious about how much available space your device has? From the Home screen, press the Menu key, scroll to highlight Options in the list of applications, and press the trackball. Scroll through the list and click Status. In the Status screen, File Free is the field that tells you how much available space is left.

A sentry is always on duty

Throughout the history of human existence, we've seen some nasty things that human beings are capable of doing. Unfortunately, the virtual world is not exempt; in fact, every day a battle is fought between those who are trying to attack a system and those who are trying to protect it. Included among those attacking the system are those who are trying to steal corporate data for their advantage, as well as individuals trying to steal personal data to carry out identity theft.

A computer connected to the Internet faces an extra risk of being hacked or becoming infected by a computer virus intent on simply annoying the heck out of you or (even worse) wreaking havoc on your computer. Fortunately, security is one of the strong points of the BlackBerry. RIM has built into its software features that allow companies to curtail activities for their BlackBerry users that they deem risky, such as installing or running a third-party application. Data transmitted on and from the device are encrypted so that possible snooping is prevented. RIM also has a Signature process for application developers, which forces developers to identify themselves and their programs if they are developing any applications running on the BlackBerry platform that need to integrate with either BlackBerry core applications or the OS.

The security measures RIM implemented on the BlackBerry platform have gained the trust of the U.S. government as well as many of the Forbes Top 500 enterprises in the financial and health industries.

Remember the *I love you* and *Anna Kournikova* viruses? These are virtual evils transmitted through e-mail, a script, or sets of instructions in the e-mail body or attachment that can be executed either by the host e-mail program or, in the case of an attachment, by the program associated with the attached file. Fortunately, BlackBerry's Messages does not support scripting languages. As for attachments, out of the box BlackBerry supports few file types, mostly images and text documents. BlackBerry's viewer for such files doesn't support scripting either, so you won't be facing threats from e-mails having these attachments.

Chapter 2

Navigating the Pearl

* *

* *

*Y*ou might have heard that the BlackBerry Pearl is different from all other BlackBerry handhelds that came before. Yes, the Pearl is a lot slimmer than other BlackBerry handhelds. Yes, it has a built-in 1.3 megapixel camera. And yes, it has a microSD memory slot. But what makes it fundamentally different is the fact that it has a trackball.

Where is the trackball? What can you do with it? How can you navigate your BlackBerry Pearl better with the trackball? Those are some of the questions that we address in this chapter. Bear with us and you will be master of your BlackBerry Pearl trackball in no time.

Anatomy 101

Together with the trackball, a few important keys will help you master navigating your BlackBerry Pearl. Figure 2-1 labels all the major keys and features on your Pearl.

The major features of your Pearl follow:

- ✔ **Display screen:** The graphical user interface (GUI) of your BlackBerry Pearl.

- ✔ **SureType keyboard:** The input for your BlackBerry Pearl.

- ✔ **Escape key:** This key is used to either cancel a selection or return to a previous page within an application (for example, the Browser).

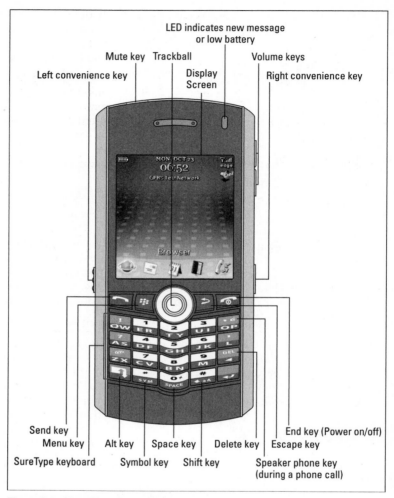

Figure 2-1: Main BlackBerry Pearl features.

✔ **Menu key:** This is used to bring up the full menu of the application you are using (see Figure 2-2, left).

If you owned a BlackBerry before, you might have noticed that the Menu key is new. The Menu key basically replaces the trackwheel click.

✔ **Trackball:** You navigate the display screen of your BlackBerry Pearl with the trackball. You have four directional movements. When you press on the trackball, a short menu of the application you're using appears (see Figure 2-2, right).

  ✓ **Left and right convenience keys:** By default, the left conven-
    ience key brings up the voice-dialing application. The right
    convenience key brings up the camera. In Chapter 3, you find
    out how to program these two keys so they bring up the pro-
    grams you use the most.

  ✓ **MicroSD slot:** Although it's hidden inside your BlackBerry
    Pearl and can be revealed only by removing the battery, your
    Pearl's microSD slot is a crucial element to your media experi-
    ence on your Pearl.

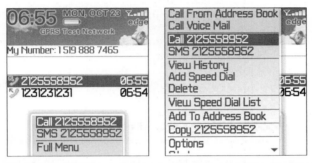

Figure 2-2: A full menu (left) and a short menu (right) in the Message application.

Display screen

When you first turn on your Pearl, the display screen displays
the *Home screen,* which is your introduction to the GUI of your
BlackBerry Pearl. The five icons represent the different applications in your BlackBerry Pearl. Refer to Figure 2-3 for examples of
what your Home screen might look like.

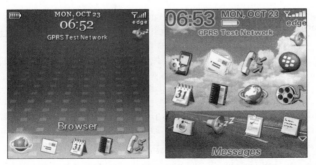

Figure 2-3: Your BlackBerry Pearl might come with a different default theme.

Depending on the theme you're using, you might see applications listed in text form rather than as icons. How your GUI looks depends on how you want it to look, because the font and theme are customizable. For more on personalizing your BlackBerry, see Chapter 3.

SureType keyboard

The Pearl doesn't have a full QWERTY keyboard. Rather, it works with a QWERTY-based keyboard known as the *SureType* keyboard. The idea here is that many keys share letters (refer to Figure 2-1) and that the SureType technology is smart enough to learn what key combinations are necessary for the words you want. Basically, with SureType, you can now type with only one thumb, and your BlackBerry Pearl learns the words that you use frequently.

Here are tips to speed up the learning curve when using SureType technology:

- ✔ **Always finish typing a word before correcting it.** This way, SureType learns what you want to type the next time.

- ✔ **If SureType got the word you're typing right on the first try, use the SPACE key to move on instead of clicking the track-ball or pressing Enter.**

- ✔ **Take advantage of Custom Wordlist, which is a list of words defined by you.** We describe this feature in a moment.

- ✔ **Type! Type! Type!** Because SureType learns how you type, the more you use it, the smarter it becomes in adapting to your style.

SureType versus multitap

On your Pearl, other than SureType, you can type in another mode: *multitap*. The regular way — at least we think of it as the regular way — is the multitap approach. The best way to explain multitap is by example: Say you want to type an **h** character on your Pearl. You search out the *h* on your keyboard but then notice to your dismay that the *h* shares a key with the letter *g*. What's a person to do? Do you really want to go through life writing *GHello* for *Hello*?

Actually, there's a perfectly easy solution to your problem. To get to the letter *g,* you tap the GH key once. To get the letter *h* — the second letter in the key's pair — you tap the key twice — hence, the term *multitap.*

To switch between multitap and SureType while you're typing, press the * key.

What about SureType? When you're in SureType mode, your Pearl tries to help you do the communication thing by figuring out what word you are typing. For example, if you want to type the word **hi**, you start by pressing the GH key and then the UI key. Doing so prompts SureType to display a list of words it thinks might be what you're aiming for, as shown in Figure 2-4.

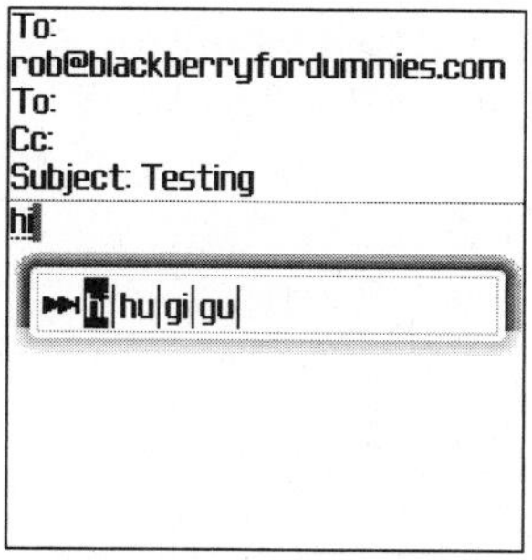

```
To:
rob@blackberryfordummies.com
To:
Cc:
Subject: Testing
hi|


  ▶▶◀hi|hu|gi|gu|
```

Figure 2-4: Now, did you want to type *hi* or *gi*?

If the first listed word is what you want, simply press the SPACE key. The word is automatically selected, and you can continue to type. If what you really wanted to type appears a little later in the list, simply scroll to it using the trackball and select it by pressing the trackball. Over time, SureType learns the words you're most likely to use and sticks those at the front of the list. Yup, that's right — it gets smarter the more you use it.

Custom Wordlist

SureType keeps all the words it has learned in a safe place — a Wordlist, to be precise. It turns out that you can review your SureType Wordlist — and even add to it — using the Custom Wordlist option. (Using this option to add words or proper names to the list means that SureType doesn't have to learn them when you're in the act of typing.)

To see or add words using the Custom Wordlist option, follow these steps:

1. **From the Home screen, press the Menu key and select Options.**

2. **Select Custom Wordlist.**

   This opens Custom Wordlist, where you can see all the words that SureType has learned. (If just got your BlackBerry recently, the list might have no words or only a few.)

3. Press the Menu key and select New.

A dialog box appears, prompting you to type a new word, as shown in Figure 2-5.

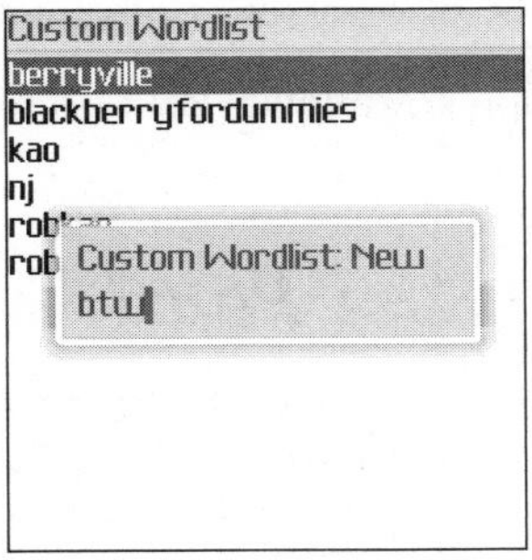

Custom Wordlist
berryville
blackberryfordummies
kao
nj
rob
rob   Custom Wordlist: New
      btw

Figure 2-5: Adding our favorite *btw* to the Custom Wordlist.

4. Type a custom word that you want to add and press the trackball.

This adds your word and saves it to the Custom Wordlist.

SureType has a tough time getting people's names right, but thankfully, you can make sure all the names in your Address Book are automatically learned by SureType by doing the following:

1. From the Home screen, press the Menu key and select Options.

2. Select Language.

You see the Language option screen, where the handy Input Option button makes its home.

3. Scroll to the Input Option button and select it.

The Fast Options screen appears with the following options:

- *Frequency Learning:* If turned on, the word used most frequently appears first in the SureType word list while you type.

- *Auto Word Learning:* If turned on, SureType learns as you type.

- *Use Address Book as Data Source:* If turned on, SureType learns all the names in your Address Book.

4. Make sure the Use Address Book as Data Source option is turned on.

If it isn't, scroll to this field, press the trackball, and select On from the drop-down list.

5. **Save your changes by pressing the Menu key and selecting Save.**

Escape key

A simple yet useful key, the Escape key allows you to return to a previous screen or cancel a selection.

Trackball — a.k.a. the Pearl

The BlackBerry Pearl got its name because of the little white translucent trackball. The trackball has two functions: scrolling and pressing. Both are described in this section.

Scrolling with your trackball

The trackball allows you to navigate the display screen in up to four directions. In a text-filled screen such as body of an e-mail, you can navigate through the text usually in all directions.

Pressing down on your trackball

Depending on where you are on the BlackBerry Pearl's screen, different situations determine what happens when you press down on the trackball, an action known as the trackball *click*:

- **Displays a drop-down list:** When you're in a choice field, pressing the trackball displays a drop-down list.

- **Confirms a choice:** The trackball can function as a confirmation key. For example, in a drop-down list, press the trackball to confirm the highlighted choice.

- **Displays a short menu:** In a text-filled screen (an e-mail body or a Web page), pressing the trackball displays a short menu (See Figure 2-2 right). The short menu is an abbreviated version of the full menu, which you can see by pressing the Menu key.

Menu key

As you can see in Figure 2-1, the Menu key is located to the left of the trackball. When you're on the Home screen, pressing the Menu key displays a popup screen listing applications installed on your BlackBerry Pearl. See Chapter 3 for instructions on how to change the order of the applications listed in the popup.

The behavior of the Menu key when the Home screen is displayed depends on the BlackBerry Pearl theme. The behavior just described is based on the default theme. To choose another theme, see Chapter 3.

When you're in an application and press the Menu key, you see the full menu for that application.

MicroSD slot

Your BlackBerry Pearl comes with 64 megabyte of memory, but a good chunk of that is taken up by applications that came with your Pearl. If you're a music or video fan, no need to worry. The folks at Research in Motion have incorporated a microSD slot in your Pearl so you can add extended memory and store all the media files you want in your BlackBerry Pearl.

At the time this book was written, a 2-gigabyte microSD card cost around $35.

To insert a microSD card, remove the battery cover and then remove the battery. Open the microSD, insert your microSD card (see Figure 2-6), and then close the microSD door. Then reinstall the battery and its cover.

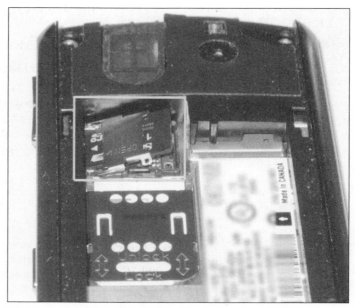

Figure 2-6: Showing a microSD card being inserted into a Pearl.

Navigation Guidelines

In the cheat sheet at the front of the book and throughout the book, we show you application-specific shortcuts. In this section, however, we go over general navigational guidelines and shortcuts. Whether you are on a Web page full of text or in an e-mail full of text, you can perform the tasks in this section.

Following are navigational basics while reading a text-filled page or a list of items, such as a list of e-mail in the Message application:

- ✔ Move to the top of the page: Press the ER key

- ✔ Move to the bottom of the page: Press the CV key

- ✔ Move to the next page: Press the M or SPACE key

- ✔ Move to the previous page: Press the UI key

- ✔ Move to the next line: Press the BN key

- ✔ Move to the previous line: Press the TY key

Following are some editing basics:

- ✔ Select a line: Press and hold the Shift key and use the trackball to scroll horizontally.

- ✔ Select multiple lines: Press and hold the Shift key and use the trackball to scroll vertically.

- ✔ Copy selected text: Press the Alt key and the trackball together.

- ✔ Cut selected text: Press the Shift and Del (delete) keys together.

- ✔ Paste text: Press the Shift key and the trackball together.

- ✔ Insert an accented letter: Hold down a letter key and horizontally scroll the trackball. As you scroll, that single letter changes on your screen. When you let go of the letter key, a list of all accents for that letter appears. You can scroll through the list to confirm the accented letter of you choice.

- ✔ Insert a symbol: Press the SYM key and select the desired symbol from the popup screen that appears.

- ✔ Num lock: Press the Shift and Alt keys together.

- ✔ Switch between multitap and SureType: When typing in a text field, press and hold the * key.

Switching applications

When you are navigating inside an application, you can quickly change applications. Just press the Menu key and select the Switch Application option. Another way to switch applications is by pressing Alt and Escape, as shown in Figure 2-7.

Figure 2-7: The switch application menu you see when you press Alt + Escape.

Changing options

Throughout the book, you'll see examples of an option field being changed to a different value. The easiest way to change the value in a field is to first scroll to the field using the trackball. Then press the trackball to see the drop-down list of choices, and finally press the trackball again on the option of your choice.

Chapter 3

Turning On Your BlackBerry Pearl (and Keeping It Happy)

*R*egardless of how long you've had your BlackBerry Pearl — one day, one week, one month — you'll want to have it around for as long as you possibly can. And, for the duration that you have your Pearl, you'll want to shine it up and make it look and sound unique. Your Pearl should reflect your personality and fashion, not someone else's.

In addition to customizing your BlackBerry Pearl so that it expresses the inner you, you want to make sure that you keep it in tip-top shape by watching out for things like battery life and information security. Luckily for you, this chapter puts any and all such worries to rest by filling you in on all you need to know to keep Pearl shiny and tuned, but yet quirkily personal.

Making Your BlackBerry Pearl Yours

The BlackBerry Pearl is the coolest toy on the market right now. The Pearl unites the sleekness of a cellular phone, the usefulness of a BlackBerry, and the versatility of a camera. Because of this terrific combination, an increasing number of people are enjoying their BlackBerry Pearl everyday. We understand your need to distinguish your BlackBerry Pearl from others'. Your wish is our command. Follow the tips and techniques outlined in this section to give your Pearl a personalized luster.

Branding your BlackBerry Pearl

Like any number of other electronic gadgets that you could possibly own, your BlackBerry Pearl comes to you off the shelf fitted out with a collection of rather white-bread factory settings. This section helps you put your name on your Pearl, both figuratively and literally. You can start by branding your name on your BlackBerry Pearl:

1. **From the Home screen, press the Menu key and select Options.**

2. **Select the Owner setting.**

   You see spaces for entering your information.

3. **In the Name field, enter your name. In the Information field, enter your contact information.**

   The idea here is to phrase a message (like the one shown in Figure 3-1) that would make sense to any possible Good Samaritan who might find your lost BlackBerry and want to return it to you.

Figure 3-1: List your owner info here.

If you lock or don't use your BlackBerry Pearl for a while, the standby screen comes on, displaying the owner information that you entered into the Options (Settings) screen. Read how to lock your BlackBerry Pearl, either manually or by using an auto setting, in "Keeping Your BlackBerry Safe," later in this chapter.

4. **Confirm your changes by pressing the Menu key and selecting Save.**

Choose a language, any language

Branding your BlackBerry Pearl with your own John Hancock is a good start, but setting the language to your native tongue so you don't need to hire a translator to use your Pearl is equally important — and equally easy. You can also set your input method of choice here, which can affect whether AutoText shows up. Don't worry. We explain what that means.

Here's how to change the language setting:

1. **From the Home screen, press the Menu key and select Options.**

2. **Select the Language setting.**

   Here you can select the language and input method of your choice.

3. **Select the Language field. In the drop-down list that appears, select your native tongue.**

   Depending on your network provider, as well as what region (North America, Europe, and so on) you're in, the language choices you have vary. Most handhelds sold in North America default to English or English (United States).

   If your network provider supports it, you can install more languages into your BlackBerry Pearl by using Application Loader in the BlackBerry Pearl Desktop Manager. For installing more languages onto your BlackBerry Pearl, contact your network service provider.

4. **Confirm your changes by pressing the Menu key and selecting Save.**

Isn't it great when you can actually read what's on the screen? But don't think that you're finished quite yet. You've still got some personalizing to do.

Typing with ease using AutoText

Your BlackBerry Pearl comes equipped with an *AutoText feature,* which is a kind of shorthand that can help you cut down on how much you have to type. AutoText basically works with a pool of abbreviations that you set up — you then type an abbreviation to get the word you associated with that abbreviation. For example, if you set *b/c* as an AutoText word for *because,* anytime you type **b/c**, you automatically get *because* onscreen.

The whole AutoText thing works only if you set up your own personal code, mapping your abbreviations to their meanings. (This is why we're discussing AutoText as part of our personalization discussion.) To set up your own code, do the following:

1. **From the Home screen, press the Menu key and select Options.**

2. **Select the AutoText option.**

   Here, you can choose to either see (or search for) existing AutoText words or create new ones.

3. **Press the Menu key and select New.**

   The AutoText screen appears, as shown in Figure 3-2.

```
AutoText: New
Replace:
b/c
With:
because
Using:              SmartCase
Language:           All Locales
```

Figure 3-2: Create AutoText here.

4. **In the Replace field, enter the characters that you want to replace (in this example, b/c). Then, in the With field, type what replaces your characters (in this example, because).**

5. **In the Using field, choose SmartCase or Specified Case.**

   • *SmartCase* capitalizes the first letter when the context calls for that, such as the first word in a sentence.

   • *Specified Case* replaces your AutoText with the exact text found in the With field.

   For example, say you have the AutoText *bbg* set up for the term *blackberryGoodies.com*, and you want it to appear as is, in terms of letter cases (the first *b* is not capitalized). If you were to choose SmartCase for this particular AutoText, it would be capitalized as the first word in a sentence, which is not what you want. On the other hand, if you use Specified Case, your AutoText always appears as *blackberryGoodies. com* no matter where it is in the sentence.

6. **Confirm your changes by pressing the Menu key and selecting Save.**

Inserting macros

If you frequently give out your BlackBerry Pearl phone number or your PIN in e-mails, you'll appreciate macros. Basically, you can use the AutoText feature to add a customized word for preset items — things like your Pearl number, PIN, or just the date — so you don't have to type them all the time.

 Keep in mind that we're talking about your BlackBerry Pearl PIN here — your device's unique identifying number — and not the PIN someone would use to empty out your checking account with the help of one of those automated tellers. For more on BlackBerry PINs, see Chapter 8.

To add a macro for your phone number, for example, first call up the AutoText screen. (AutoText is one of the options in Options [Settings].) Type an appropriate word in the Replace field (*mynum* would work nicely), scroll to the With field, press the Menu key, select Insert Macro, and then press the trackball. You're prompted with a popup to select from a list of preset items; be sure to scroll to the Phone Number (%p) option.

After saving your setting, you can test your AutoText by drafting a simple e-mail.

Getting your dates and times lined up

Having the correct date, time, and time zone is important when it comes to your BlackBerry Pearl for obvious reasons, we hope. When it comes to having the correct time, the easiest way is to let BlackBerry Pearl adjust it for you. How? Your Pearl can automatically set its time by using your network provider's server time. This way, you need not worry about daylight saving time.

However, even when using your network service provider's time, you still need to set up your time zone properly. Follow these steps:

1. **From the Home screen, press the Menu key and select Options.**

2. **Select the Date/Time setting.**

    The Date/Time screen appears.

3. **Select the Time Zone field. In the drop-down list that appears, select Change Option.**

   A drop-down list of time zones appears.

4. **Select your time zone.**

   The Date/Time screen confirms the time zone that you select.

5. **Select the Date/Time Source field.**

   A drop-down list of sources appears, as shown in Figure 3-3.

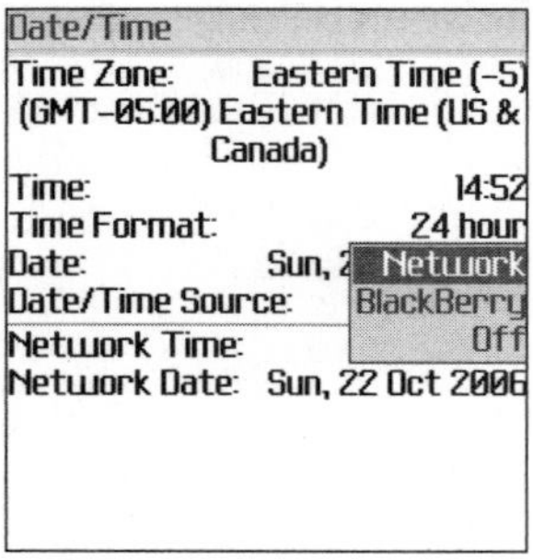

```
Date/Time
Time Zone:      Eastern Time (-5)
(GMT-05:00) Eastern Time (US &
              Canada)
Time:                       14:52
Time Format:             24 hour
Date:          Sun, 2  Network
Date/Time Source:   BlackBerry
Network Time:               Off
Network Date:  Sun, 22 Oct 2006
```

Figure 3-3: Set the time source of your Pearl to your network provider's clock.

6. **Select Network.**

   This sets your service provider's server time as your date and time source.

7. **Confirm your changes by pressing the Menu key and selecting Save.**

   Doing so saves your date and time settings in perpetuity — a really long time, in other words.

Customizing your screen's look and feel

Right up there with making sure that your date and time settings are accurate is getting the display font, font size, and screen contrast to your liking. Now we know that some of you don't give a hoot if your fonts are Batang or Bookman as long as you can read the text, but we also know that some of you won't stop configuring the fonts until you get them absolutely right. For all you tweakers out there, here's how you play around with your BlackBerry Pearl fonts:

1. **From the Home screen, press the Menu key and select Options.**

2. **Select the Screen/Keyboard setting.**

   The Screen/Keyboard screen appears with various customizable fields, as shown in Figure 3-4.

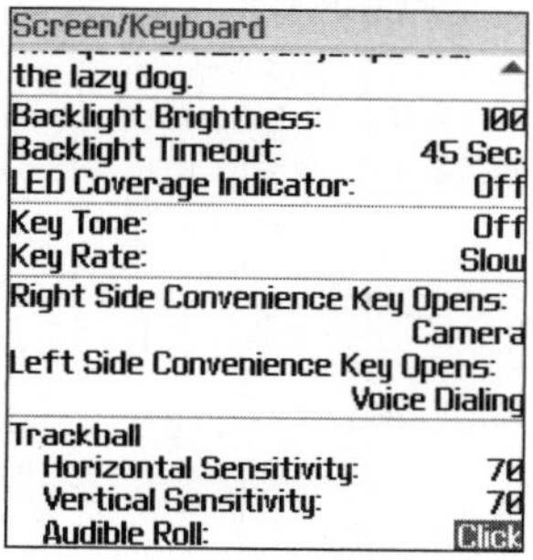

Figure 3-4: The Screen/Keyboard screen, waiting for personalization.

3. **Select the Font Family field. In the drop-down list that appears, select the font you want.**

   In the drop-down list, you'll find three to ten fonts, depending on your provider.

4. **Select the Font Size field. In the drop-down list that appears, select the font size you want.**

   The smaller the font size, the more you can see onscreen; however, a smallish font is harder on the eyes.

   Note: As you scroll up and down the list of fonts and font sizes, notice that the text "The quick brown fox jumps over the lazy dog" takes on the look of the selected font and size so that you can preview what the particular font looks like before you confirm your selection.

5. **Confirm your changes by pressing the Menu key and selecting Save.**

Tuning Pearl navigation

With fonts out of the way, it's time to fine-tune the Pearl so that it navigates the way you want it to. To help you get to the applications that you need the most, the folks at Research in Motion have created two convenience keys that bring up applications.

To configure these convenience keys, follow these steps:

1. **From the Home screen, press the Menu key and select Options.**

2. **Select the Screen/Keyboard setting.**

   The Screen/Keyboard screen appears with its various customizable fields (refer to Figure 3-4).

3. **Select the Right Side Convenience Key Opens field. In the drop-down list that appears, select the application you want.**

   For example, instead of the default camera, you can have your right side convenience key launch your browser.

4. **Select the Left Side Convenience Key Opens field. In the drop-down list that appears, select the application you want.**

   You can select what you want your left side key to open when you press it.

   If you often multitask on your BlackBerry Pearl, you can configure one of your convenience keys to be the Application Switcher. This way, you can easily switch from, say, e-mailing to browsing.

5. **Select the Trackball Horizontal Sensitivity field. In the drop-down list that appears, select an option.**

   This option determines how sensitive you want the trackball to be horizontally. You can choose anywhere from 20 to 100 for this option, where 20 is the least sensitive and 100 is the most sensitive.

6. **Select the Trackball Vertical Sensitivity field. In the drop-down list that appears, select an option.**

   This option is like the preceding one, only it determines the trackball's vertical movement. Keep in mind that if your trackball is too sensitive, it will be hard to control. On the other hand, if your trackball is not sensitive enough, you might find it slow.

   Think of trackball sensitivity settings as the mouse sensitivity on the PC. The right sensitivity can be helpful for making the trackball go exactly where you want it. Play around with vertical and horizontal sensitivities and adjust them to your liking.

7. **Confirm your changes by pressing the Menu key and selecting Save.**

Choosing themes for your BlackBerry

Your BlackBerry Pearl is preloaded with different *themes* depending on your provider (see Figure 3-5). To change your theme, follow these steps:

1. **From the Home screen, press the Menu key and select Options.**

2. **Select the Theme setting.**

   You see a list of available Themes.

3. **Select the Theme you want.**

   You see a preview of the theme you've selected.

4. **Select Activate from the contextual menu that appears.**

   You should see the change immediately.

Figure 3-5: Two different themes on a BlackBerry Pearl.

You can always download other themes here — just remember that you have to use your BlackBerry, not your PC, to access these URLs:

- http://mobile.blackberry.com
- www.blackberrygoodies.com/bb/themes

Unlike the figure on the left in Figure 3-5, your BlackBerry Pearl, out of the box, probably doesn't come with a theme that lists all applications on the Home screen. To see the list of applications installed on your BlackBerry Pearl, you need to press the Menu key to see the Application List, as shown in Figure 3-6. We know what you are thinking: What if you don't like the order in which applications are listed in the Application List? Don't worry, you can change that order — and hide the applications you don't often use.

Figure 3-6: Popup showing a list of applications.

To change the order of the applications in the Application List:

1. **From the Home screen, press the Menu key.**

   This brings up a popup showing a list of applications.

2. **If you have the T-Mobile Zen Theme, select the Organize Applications option.**

3. **Scroll to the desired application, press the Menu key, and select Move Application.**

   Doing this allows you to scroll the desired application up and down throughout the list, as shown in Figure 3-7.

Figure 3-7: A Browser application is being moved.

4. **Move the trackball up and down to place the application into the desired order, and then press the trackball.**

   This completes the ordering of the application that you selected in Step 3.

To hide an application, select Hide Application instead of Move Application in Step 3. A grayed icon means it is currently hidden.

The first five applications listed in the Application List screen are the ones accessible from your Home screen. So choose your top five listed applications based on what you do the most on your BlackBerry Pearl.

Wallpaper for your BlackBerry

Like your desktop PC, you can customize your BlackBerry to have personalized wallpaper for your Home screen. You can set an image to be your BlackBerry Home screen background by using the BlackBerry Media application, as follows:

1. **From the Home screen, press the Menu key and select Media.**

   The Media application opens, and you see several categories: Music, Video, Ringtones, and Pictures.

2. **Select the Picture category.**

   Doing so brings up two folders named Preloaded Media and Device Memory. The Preloaded Media folder stores pictures that came with your BlackBerry Pearl, and the Device Memory folder stores pictures that you took with your camera.

3. **Select the Preloaded Media folder.**

   You see all the pictures in the folder. If you've taken pictures with the BlackBerry Pearl camera (see Chapter 11), you might want to use the Device Memory folder instead.

4. **Select the picture you want to use for your home screen background**

   The selected picture appears in full-screen view.

5. **Press the Menu key and select Set as Home Screen Image.**

   The picture is set as your new Home screen wallpaper.

6. **Press and hold the Escape key to return to the Home screen to see the result.**

The Escape key is located on the right side of the trackball. For more on the BlackBerry Pearl's body features, see Chapter 2.

You can download free wallpaper at the following:

- ✒ http://mobile.blackberry.com
- ✒ www.blackberrywallpapers.com
- ✒ www.blackberrygoodies.com/bb/wallpapers

Remember that you need to use your BlackBerry, not your PC, to access these URLs.

After you have your BlackBerry's look and feel just the way you want, there's just one thing left to do before you can move on: getting your BlackBerry to *sound* the way you want it to.

Let freedom ring

The whole appeal of the BlackBerry phenomenon is the idea that this little electronic device can make your life easier. One of the ways it accomplishes this is by acting as your personal reminder service — letting you know when an appointment is coming up, a phone call is coming in, an e-mail has arrived, and so on. Basically, your BlackBerry is set to bark at you if it feels there's something it knows that you should know. Figure 3-8 lists the kinds of things your BlackBerry considers bark-worthy, ranging from browser alerts to tasks deadlines.

Figure 3-8: Set attention-needy applications here.

People react differently to different sounds. Some BlackBerry barks would be greatly appreciated by certain segments of the population, whereas other segments might react to the same sound by pitching their BlackBerry under the nearest bus. The folks at Research in Motion are well aware of this fact and have devised a great way for you to customize how you want your BlackBerry to bark at you — they call it your *profile*.

You can jump right into things by using a predefined profile, or you can create your own profile. The upcoming sections look at both approaches.

Whether you create your own profile or customize a predefined profile, each profile is divided into different categories. Each category is really just the application for which you want to define an alert. The following is a sample list of applications that you can define within each profile:

- ✔ **Browser:** Alerts you when you receive a new *channel push,* which is just a Web page sent to your BlackBerry.

- ✔ **Calendar:** Alerts you when you have upcoming appointments.

- ✔ **Level1 Messages (urgent e-mail messages):** Alerts you with a special tone when you have an urgent e-mail. What's considered an urgent message? E-mail can be defined as urgent by your sender. Also, a BlackBerry PIN-to-PIN message can be considered urgent. For more on PIN-to-PIN, see Chapter 8.

- ✔ **Messages:** Alerts you when there is a new e-mail message in your inbox.

- ✔ **Phone:** Alerts you if there is an incoming call or a new voice mail.

- ✔ **SMS:** Alerts you when you have an SMS message.

- ✔ **Tasks:** Alerts you of an upcoming to-do deadline.

 You might have more categories than what we've listed here. For example, if your Pearl came with the Instant Messaging program, you might have New IM — AIM and New IM — Yahoo! on your list. Regardless how many categories you have, configure them the same way as described in this section.

You can personalize all the listed applications depending on how you want to be alerted. Because the way you customize them is similar, we use the Message application as an example in the text that follows, as we customize a predefined profile that comes with your BlackBerry.

After this, we go over creating a new profile from scratch. You might be wondering: Why do I need to create a new profile if I can personalize the predefined profiles? Well, if you want to keep the predefined settings the way they are and heavily personalize your profile, creating a new profile is the way to go.

Using factory settings

If you're okay with customizing a predefined, factory-loaded profile, do the following:

 1. From the Home screen, press the Menu key and select Profile.

A screen listing all the profiles appears, as shown in Figure 3-9.

2. Select Advanced.

Figure 3-9: List of profiles for you to choose from.

3. Scroll to the Normal profile in the list, press the Menu key, and select Edit.

The Normal screen appears, listing the different applications with alert capabilities (refer to Figure 3-8).

4. In the Normal screen, select the Messages application. Then select the Edit option.

You're faced with the Messages configure screen, which is divided into an Out of Holster section and an In Holster section, as shown in Figure 3-10. A *holster* (in this context) is simply the belt-clip or case that houses your BlackBerry while you're not using it. BlackBerry is smart enough to know when it's in a holster.

```
Messages[Email] in Normal
Out of Holster:                    None
Tune:              No             Tone
Volume:                          Vibrate
Number of Beeps:            Vibrate+Tone
Repeat Notification:      LED Flashing
Number of Vibrations:                2
In Holster:                      Vibrate
Tune:                   Notifier_Nymph
Volume:                             Mute
Number of Beeps:                       1
Repeat Notification:      LED Flashing
Number of Vibrations:                2
```

Figure 3-10: Choose a tone to alert you when your BlackBerry is out of its holster.

5. Select the Out of Holster field, and then select the Change Option.

You're prompted with a drop-down list, spelling out your alert options.

6. **Select Tone.**

   Doing so enables sound in the Out of Holster mode.

7. **Continuing in the Message configure screen, select the Tune field. Then select Change Option.**

   You're prompted with a set of tunes in a drop-down list. *Note:* You're not going to find "Stairway to Heaven" here, but you should be able to find something you like. If you can't find one you like, you can always download ringtones; see Chapter 12 for more information.

8. **Select the tune you'd like.**

   As you scroll through the tunes and pause, BlackBerry plays the tune so you know what it sounds like before you change it.

9. **Confirm your changes by pressing the trackball and selecting Save.**

As you might have guessed from how the Messages in Default screen is divided, your BlackBerry can notify you in different ways based on whether your BlackBerry is in plain view (Out of Holster) or tucked away next to your belt (In Holster). To set up a different sound for In Holster mode, just put the necessary info in the fields for the In Holster section — and be sure to choose a different tune this time. (Choosing the same tune kind of defeats the purpose, doesn't it?)

As we mentioned, you can do the same to personalize other applications listed in each profile.

If you're like us and you get more than 200 e-mails a day, you probably don't want your BlackBerry sounding off each time an e-mail arrives. What you can do is set up your BlackBerry so that it notifies you only if an e-mail has been marked as *urgent,* requiring your immediate attention. Set the notification for your Messages application to None for both In Holster and Out of Holster. Then, in the Level1 Messages option, set your desired notification for both In Holster and Out of Holster. That way, you have conveniently filtered any unnecessary e-mail notifications, leaving just the urgent stuff to sound off to you.

Creating your own profile

You need to know which applications on your BlackBerry have alert capabilities because you can then personalize each "Hey, you!" to your liking. You can have your BlackBerry so personalized that you can tell whether you have a phone call or an incoming message just by how your BlackBerry sounds.

If you're already familiar with the different applications and are clear how you want each one to alert you, go on and create your own profile. As we mentioned, you can achieve the same result by personalizing the predefined profiles that come with your BlackBerry. But if you are one of those who likes to keep the predefined profiles the way they are, go ahead and create a new profile.

1. **From the Home screen, press the Menu key and select profile.**

   A popup screen listing all the profiles appears (refer to Figure 3-9).

2. **Select Advanced.**

3. **Press the Menu key and select New Profile (see Figure 3-11).**

   A new Profiles screen appears, prompting you to name your profile.

```
Profiles
Loud
Vibrate
Quiet
Normal (Active)
Phone Only
Off
Use Active Profile Except For:
  ☑ Important Calls
New Profile
New Exception
Edit
Show Tunes
Switch Application
Close
```

Figure 3-11: Creating your own profile.

4. **In the Name field, enter a name for your profile.**

   For this example, just type **My Profile**.

5. **Configure your new profile.**

   Refer to Steps 3 through 7 of the preceding "Using factory settings" section to customize each one of the seven applications.

6. **Press the trackball and select Save.**

   Your newly created Profile appears listed in the Profiles screen.

7. **In the Profiles screen, select My Profile and press the trackball.**

   This activates your newly created profile and returns you to the Home screen.

Regardless whether the ringtone is for an incoming call or an incoming e-mail, you can download more ringtones to personalize your BlackBerry.

You can download free ringtones at `mobile.blackberry.com`. Just be sure to call up this URL with your BlackBerry, not your PC.

To switch between the current profile and a vibrating profile: From the Home screen, press and hold the # key.

Creating an exception

What is an exception? An exception assigns a specific ringtone to a particular person's phone number(s) in the Address Book. For example, say your current ringtone for any phone call is the default ringtone, but you want calls from your significant other to be some romantic song. One way to do this is to create an exception. Another way is to have a custom ringtone set for a contact in your Address Book; refer to Chapter 4 for details on that method.

To create a new exception, choose New Exception instead of New profile in Step 3 of the preceding section. You'll see a screen similar to Figure 3-12. Choose the From field from your Address Book. Please note that exceptions apply only to phone calls.

Figure 3-12: Creating an exception for the Quiet profile.

Power Usage and Consumption

Your BlackBerry Pearl comes equipped with a rechargeable, replaceable lithium battery that can have *stand-by time* (time when your BlackBerry is on but not being used) that lasts around 10 to 15 days. The more you use the *backlight* (the light that lets you see your display screen better), the more quickly your battery is going to run out. Finally, keep in mind that your BlackBerry Pearl is an

Internet-ready device (okay, okay, we know you know that, because that's why you got it, right?) and that anything you do with a network signal (sending and receiving e-mails, Internet browsing, talking on the phone) eats into your battery reserves in a big way.

Here is a handy list of battery conservation tips to keep your BlackBerry up and running as long as possible while you're on the go:

- **Reduce backlight amount and timeout.** Using the Screen/ Keyboard option, adjust your backlight to a low setting. In addition, set the backlight timeout as low as possible. (You can get the details on setting Screen/Keyboard option in the "Customizing your screen's look and feel" section, earlier in this chapter.)

- **Don't use what you don't need.** Turn off any wireless capabilities if you're in an area where you're out of coverage (for example, underground or on an airplane) so that your Pearl doesn't waste its battery searching for radio signals. (For all the details on dealing with wireless features, see Part III.)

  Since your Pearl has Bluetooth capability, turn it off during those times when you have no use for it.

- **Bulk up your power.** If you are a heavy phone user or are on the go all the time, consider purchasing an extra extended battery or a car power kit. See Chapter 16, where we suggest where to purchase one.

Keeping Your BlackBerry Safe

The folks at Research in Motion take security seriously, and so should you. Always set up a password on your BlackBerry Pearl. If your Pearl hasn't prompted you to set up a password, you should immediately do so. Here's how:

1. **Press the Menu key and select Security Options.**

2. **Select General Settings.**

   The Security screen appears.

3. **Select the Password field and, in the drop-down list that appears, select Enabled.**

   All this does for now is enable the Password feature. You won't be prompted to type a password until you save the changes you just made.

4. **Confirm your changes by pressing the Menu key and selecting Save.**

   At this time, you should be prompted for a password.

5. **Type a password and then type it again for verification.**

   From this point on, whenever you lock your BlackBerry Pearl and want to use it again, you have to type the same password. How to lock your BlackBerry? Good question, keep reading.

Make sure to remember what your password is and not just which key you press. You need the same password if you link your BlackBerry Pearl with the BlackBerry Desktop Manager for synchronization. For more on BlackBerry Desktop Manager, please refer to Chapter 13.

Setting up your password is a good first step, but just having a password won't help you much if you don't take the further step of locking your BlackBerry when you're not using it. (You don't want people at the office or sitting at the next table at the coffee shop checking out your e-mails or phone history when you take a bathroom break, do you?) So, how do you lock your BlackBerry? Let us count the ways. We came up with two, in fact.

You can go the Autolock After Timeout (also known as Security Timeout) route:

1. **Press the Menu key and select Options.**

2. **Select the Security option.**

3. **Select General Settings.**

   The Security screen appears.

4. **Select the Security Timeout field and, in the drop-down list that appears, select the desired time.**

   The preset times range from 1 minute to 1 hour.

5. **Confirm your changes by pressing the Menu key and selecting Save.**

To lock your Pearl on demand, simply press and hold the asterisk (*) key when you're on the Home screen. You probably would lock your Pearl if you want to prevent others from accessing your data or before you put your Pearl into your pocket.

No matter what route you take to lock your Blackberry Pearl, you use your (newly created) password to unlock it when you get back from wherever you've been.

Who Ya Gonna Call (When Your BlackBerry Pearl Breaks)?

Certainly not those Ghostbusters guys. We do suggest that you contact your network service provider first. (Remember them? They're the guys who sold you the device in the first place.)

You can't buy direct from RIM! Is that true? Before you start calling anyone, you should know that your BlackBerry Pearl, holster, and cradle (if it came with one) are under a one-year warranty from either RIM itself or your service provider. Within the first year, RIM or your service provider will replace or repair your BlackBerry if any defect is found. Do keep in mind, though, that your warranty does not cover any damage to your Pearl caused by an accident or misuse.

With that out of the way, if your BlackBerry Pearl is still under the one-year warranty and it somehow isn't functioning properly, give your service provider a ring. (Table 3-1 lists the customer service numbers of the major U.S. and Canadian service providers.)

Table 3-1 Toll-Free Numbers for Major Service Providers

Network Service Provider	Customer Support Number
T-Mobile	1-800-937-8997
Verizon	1-800-922-0204
Cingular/AT&T	1-800-331-0500/1-866-293-4634
Rogers AT&T (Canada)	1-866-931-3282
Telus (Canada)	1-866-558-2273

If your Pearl is out of warranty, you can have it repaired or replaced for a fee. The best bet is still to contact your network service provider to find out how much it would cost to repair it, and to find out whether you have other options.

Part II
Getting Organized with Your Pearl

The 5th Wave   By Rich Tennant

"Okay antidote, antidote, what would an antidote icon look like? You know, I still haven't got this desktop the way I'd like it."

In this part . . .

This part covers how to use your BlackBerry to its fullest to get you — and keep you — organized. Peruse the chapters here to find out how to use your Address Book, keep appointments, make notes, and keep your passwords safe.

Chapter 4

Remembering and Locating Your Acquaintances

*T*he idea of an address book was around long before the BlackBerry was conceived. Address Book on the BlackBerry serves the same function as any address book: an organizational tool that gives you a place to record information about people. This tool gives you a central place from which you can retrieve information so that you can reach your contacts through many ways: phone, cellphone, e-mail, and snail mail. In today's environment, an address book is an essential tool, and your BlackBerry is there at the ready.

In this chapter, we show you how to make your BlackBerry a handy, timesaving tool for managing your contacts' information. Specifically, you find out how to add, change, and delete contacts as well as how to locate them later. You'll also be amazed at how well the Address Book is integrated with all the other BlackBerry features you've come to know and love — phoning contacts, adding invites to your meetings, adding contacts to BlackBerry Messenger, and composing e-mails.

Accessing Your Address Book

 The good people at Research in Motion make it easy for you to find the Address Book. Start by taking a look at the BlackBerry Home screen. The Address Book icon looks like a little black book.

Opening the Address Book couldn't be simpler: Use the trackball to highlight its icon and then press the trackball or press Enter.

Any application menu is always accessible through the Menu key.

Working with Address Book Names

You have a new BlackBerry. The first thing you'll want to do is try to call or e-mail someone, right? But wait a sec — you don't have any contact information yet, which means you're going to have to type in someone's e-mail address each time you send an e-mail — a hassle if there ever were one.

Time to get with the plan. Most of us humans — social creatures that we are — maintain a list of contacts somewhere, whether in an old cellphone, or maybe on a piece of paper tucked away in a wallet. We're pretty sure you have some kind of list somewhere. The trick is getting that list into your BlackBerry device so that you can access the info more efficiently. The good news for you is that the "getting contact info into your BlackBerry device" trick isn't a hard one to master. Stick with us, and you'll have it down pat by the end of this chapter.

Often the simplest way to get contact information into your BlackBerry is to enter it manually. However, if you've invested a lot of time and energy in maintaining some type of address book application on your desktop computer, you might want to hot sync that data into your BlackBerry. Chapter 13 provides details on how to synchronize some of your desktop application data — address book, e-mail, appointments, and memos stuff.

Creating a new contact

Have you tried chanting someone's phone number because you can't scare up a writing implement? Not if you have your handy BlackBerry device with you. With BlackBerry in hand, follow these steps to create a new contact:

1. **From the Address Book screen, press the Menu key and select New Address.**

   The New Address screen appears, as shown in Figure 4-1 (left).

New Address	Find:
Title:	Abraham Lincoln
First: ‖	Benjamin Franklin
Last:	Dante Sarigumba
Picture:	**Jane Doe, XYZ Corporation**
[figure]	
Email:	
Company:	
Job Title:	
Work:	
Work 2: ▼	

Figure 4-1: Create a new contact (left). Address Book after adding Jane Doe (right).

2. **Scroll through the various fields, stopping and entering the contact information you feel is appropriate.**

   You'll use your BlackBerry keyboard to enter this information.

3. **When you finish entering the contact information you want, press the Menu key and select Save.**

   At this point, you should see your Jane Doe added to the list, as shown in Figure 4-1 (right).

A word from the seers

We don't think you can overdo it when entering a person's contact information. You should strive to enter complete information or as much as you possibly can. Maybe the benefit won't be obvious now, but in the future when your memory fails or your boss needs a critical piece of info that you just so happen to have at the ready, you'll thank us for this advice.

To create another new blank e-mail field for the same contact, press the Menu key and select Add Email Address. You can have up to three e-mail addresses per contact.

When entering an e-mail address, press the SPACE key to insert an @ symbol or a period (.).

If a contact has an extension for his or her phone number, no problem. When calling such a contact from your BlackBerry, you can instruct BlackBerry to dial the extension after the initial phone number. When entering the phone number into the New Address or Enter Address screen, type the primary phone number, press the Menu key, select Add Wait or Add Pause from the menu that appears, and then add the extension number. Wait lets your BlackBerry know that it's time to call up the Extension Dialog screen, which prompts you to enter the extension number. Pause tells your BlackBerry to dial the extension number for you — after a two-second delay — whenever you want it to.

Adding your own fields

Perhaps your contact information really doesn't fit into any of the available fields. Although you can't really create any additional fields from scratch, you can commandeer one of the User fields for your own purposes.

The User fields are located at the bottom of the screen — you have to scroll down to see them. Basically, the User fields are fair game — you can use these fields any way you want (which is great), and you can even change the field's name. (Face it, *User field* is not that helpful as a descriptive title.) For example, you could rename User fields to capture suffixes (such as MD, PhD, and so on). Or how about profession, birth date, hobbies, school, or nickname? When it comes down to it, you decide what information is important to you. Just remember that changing a User field name applies to the entire Address Book and not just one contact.

To rename a User field:

1. **Scroll to the bottom of the screen to navigate to one of the User fields.**

2. **Press the Menu key and select Change Field Name.**

   Note: The Change Field Name selection appears only if the cursor is in a User field.

3. **Use the keyboard to enter the new User field name.**

4. **To save your changes, press the trackball or Enter key.**

   You're all set.

Adding contacts from other BlackBerry applications

When you receive an e-mail message or get a call from someone, you've got yourself some contact information in Messages or Phone. (RIM makes this easy for you because Messages and Phone can recognize phone numbers or e-mail addresses and then highlight that information for a quick cut and paste.) Maybe that info isn't complete, but you definitely have at least an e-mail address or a phone number to start with. Now, if you're pretty sure you'll be corresponding with this person, it's just logical that you'd want to add that information to your BlackBerry Address Book.

When you have an e-mail or a phone log open, just scroll to an e-mail address or phone number and press the Menu key while that piece of information is highlighted. An Add to Address Book option pops up on the menu. Select Add to Address Book, and a New Address screen appears, prefilled with that particular piece of information. All you need to do now is enter the rest of the information you know about the person, ready to be saved into the Address Book — just one more sign of BlackBerry's ongoing attempt to make your life easier.

Viewing a contact

Okay, you just entered your friend's name, *Jane,* into your BlackBerry, but you have this nagging thought in the back of your mind that you typed the wrong phone number. You want to quickly view Jane's information. Just highlight Jane's name from the Address Book list screen and press the trackball. Pressing the trackball while a name is highlighted is the same as opening the menu and selecting View — just quicker.

View mode displays only information that's been filled in. (It doesn't bother showing fields in which you haven't entered anything.)

Editing a contact

Change is an inevitable part of life. Given that fact, your contact information is sure to change as well. If you want to keep the information you diligently put in your Address Book current, you'll have to do some updating now and then.

To update a contact, follow these steps:

1. **From the Address Book list screen, highlight the contact name you want to edit, press the Menu key, and select Edit.**

   The Edit Address screen for the contact name you selected makes an appearance.

2. **Scroll through the various fields of the Edit Address screen, editing the contact information as you see fit.**

If you want to replace only a few words or letters located in the middle of a field (rather than replacing the whole text), hold down the Alt key while scrolling the trackball to position your cursor precisely on the text you want to change. Then make your desired changes.

3. Press the Menu key and select Save.

The edit you made for this contact is saved.

 When you're editing information and you want to totally replace the entry with a new one, it is much faster to first clear the contents, especially if the old data is long. When you are in an editable field (as opposed to a selectable field), just press the Menu key and then select the Clear Field option. This feature is available in all text-entry fields and for most BlackBerry applications.

Deleting a contact

When it's time to eradicate somebody's contact information (whether a case of duplication, or a bit of bad blood — yes, we admit to having occasionally stricken someone from our Address Books in a fit of pique), the BlackBerry OS makes it easy. Just highlight the contact name you want to delete from the Address Book list screen and press the DEL key. When you're ready to part with this record, click Delete from the confirmation screen. That's it. The contact is deleted and disappears from your contact list.

 Sometimes dealing with the Confirmation screen can be a pain if you want to delete several contacts in a row. If you are 100 percent sure that you want to ditch a number of contacts, you can suspend the Confirmation feature by setting the Confirm Delete option to No in the Address Book Options screen. Check the "Setting preferences" section later in this chapter for more on Address Book options.

Looking for Someone?

Somehow — usually through a combination of typing skills and the shuttling of data between various electronic devices — you've created a nice long list of contacts in your Address Book. Nice enough, we suppose, but useless unless you can find the phone number of Rufus T. Firefly at the drop of a hat.

That's where the Find screen comes in. In fact, the first thing that you see in the Address Book when you open it is the Find screen, as shown in the left screen of Figure 4-2.

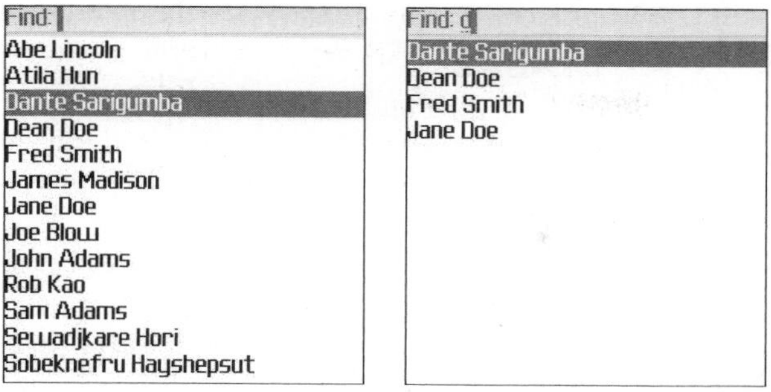

Find:		Find: d
Abe Lincoln		Dante Sarigumba
Atila Hun		Dean Doe
Dante Sarigumba		Fred Smith
Dean Doe		Jane Doe
Fred Smith		
James Madison		
Jane Doe		
Joe Blow		
John Adams		
Rob Kao		
Sam Adams		
Sewadjkare Hori		
Sobeknefru Hayshepsut		

Figure 4-2: Your search starts here (left). Enter letters to shorten the potential contact list search (right).

You can conveniently search through your contacts by following these steps:

1. **In the Find field, enter the starting letters of the name you want to search for.**

   Your search criterion is the name of the person. You could enter the last name or first name or both.

    The list is usually sorted by first name and then last name. As you type the letters, notice that the list starts shrinking based on the matches on the letters you enter. The right screen in Figure 4-2 illustrates how this works.

2. **Highlight the name from the list of matches.**

   If you have multiple matches, use the trackball to scroll through the list to find the person's name.

3. **Press the Menu key and select from the possible actions listed on the menu that appears.**

   After you find the person you want, you can select from these options, some of which are shown in Figure 4-3:

   - *Email:* Starts a new e-mail message. See Chapter 7 for more information about e-mail.

   - *PIN:* Starts a new PIN-to-PIN message, which is a messaging system unique to BlackBerry. With PIN-to-PIN, you can send someone who has a BlackBerry a quick message. See Chapter 8 for more details about PIN-to-PIN messaging.

   - *Call:* Uses the phone to dial the number.

   - *SMS:* Starts a new SMS message. SMS is short for *Short Messaging Service,* which is used in cellphones. See Chapter 8 for more details about SMS.

- *Send to Messenger Contact:* Send this Address entry to one of your BlackBerry Messenger contacts.

- *MMS:* Short for Multimedia Messaging Service, an evolution of SMS that allows you to send multimedia messages, such as audio and video clips. See Chapter 8 for more details on MMS.

Figure 4-3: You get options for the selected contact.

If you have a finger-fumble and press a letter key in error, press the Escape key once to return to the original list (the one showing all your contacts), or press the Menu key once and select View All.

 If you think you're hallucinating when you notice that sometimes the menu item `Email <contact name>` or `Call <contact name>` displays on the menu and sometimes not, relax. There's nothing wrong with your eyesight or your mind. Address Book is smart enough to know when it's appropriate to show those menu options. If a contact has a phone number, `Call <contact name>` and `SMS <contact name>` show up, and the same is true for e-mail and personal identification number (PIN). In fact, this list of actions is a convenient way to find out if you have particular information — a phone number or an e-mail address — for a contact.

 If you have a long list in your Address Book and you want to scroll down a page at a time, just hold down the Alt key and scroll. You'll get where you need to go a lot faster.

Organizing Your Contacts

You've been diligent by adding your contacts to your Address Book, and your list has been growing at a pretty good clip. It now has all the contact information for your business colleagues, clients, and (of course) family, friends, and relatives. In fact, your Address Book has grown so much that it now holds hundreds of contacts, and you start to notice that it now takes you more time to find somebody.

You know this isn't rocket science. You're going to want to do one of the following:

✔ **Organize your contacts into groups.** Using groups (as every kindergarten teacher could tell you) is a way to arrange something (in your case, contacts) to make them more manageable. How you arrange your groups is really up to you because the organizing principle should be based on whatever makes sense (to you, at least) and fits the group you set up. For example, you can place all your customer contacts in a Clients group and family members and relatives in a Family group. Then, instead of searching for names of individuals in one humongous list, you can search in a smaller, more manageable group.

✔ **Set up your contacts so that you can use some kind of filter on them.** Another way to organize and streamline how your BlackBerry Address Book lists your contacts is to use the Filter feature in combination with BlackBerry's Categories. (*Categories* is just another way BlackBerry Address Book helps you filter your contacts.) Using the Filter feature narrows the Address Book list to such an extent that you have to use only trackball to scroll down and find your contact — no need to type search keywords.

Whether you use the Group or Filter feature is up to you. You'll find out how to use both methods in the next sections.

Creating a group

A BlackBerry group in Address Book — as opposed to any other kind of group you can imagine — is just a simple filter or category. In other words, a *group* arranges your contacts into subsets without affecting the content of your contact entries. In the Address Book itself, a group shows up in the contact list just like any other contact. The only wrinkle here is that when you select the group, the contacts associated with that group — and *only* the contacts associated with that group — appear onscreen.

Need some help visualizing how this works? Go ahead and create a new group, following these steps:

1. **From the Address Book screen, press the Menu key and select New Group.**

   A screen appears, allowing you to enter a group name.

2. **In the New Group field, enter the name of the group.**

   You could name the group anything, but for the sake of this example, go ahead and name the group *Friends*.

   After entering the name of the group, you're ready to save it. But hold on a sec — you can't save this group until you associate a member to it. To satisfy such a hard-and-fast rule, proceed to the next step to add a member.

3. **Press the Menu key and select Add Member.**

   The main Address Book list shows up in all its glory, ready to be pilfered for names to add to your new Group list.

4. **Highlight the name of a contact you want to add to your new Group list. Then press the trackball and make a selection from the menu that appears.**

   You can select from these options:

   - *Email:* Adds the contact's e-mail address to the group.
   - *PIN:* Adds the contact's PIN to the group.
   - *Phone:* Adds the contact's phone number to the group.

   Everybody knows a Rob Kao, so go ahead and select him. You'll notice that doing so places Rob Kao in your Friends group list, as shown in Figure 4-4. (Rob Kao, a co-author of the book you're holding in your hands, is a very popular fellow.)

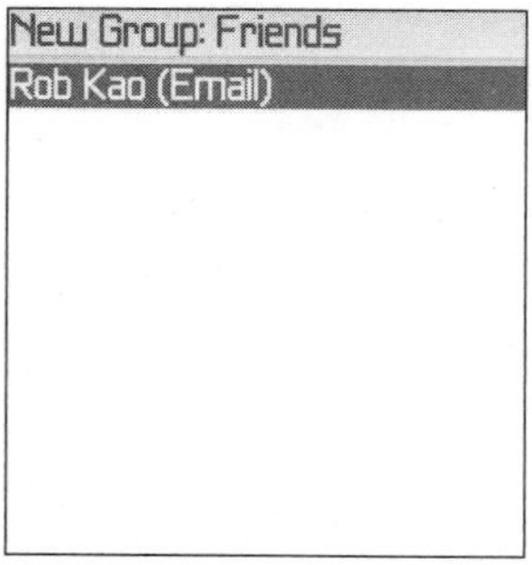

Figure 4-4: Your new group has one member.

5. **Repeat Steps 3 and 4 to add more friends to your list.**

   After you're satisfied, save your group.

6. **Press the Menu key and select Save Group.**

   Your Friends group is duly saved, and you can now see Friends listed on your main Address Book list.

Using the Filter feature on your contacts

Are you a left-brainer or a right-brainer? Yankees fan or Red Sox fan? An innie or an outie? Dividing up the world into categories is something everybody does (no divisions there), so it should come as no surprise that BlackBerry divides your contacts into distinct categories as well.

By default, two categories are already set for you on your BlackBerry: the Business category and the Personal category. But why stop at two? BlackBerry makes it easy to create more categories. In this section, you first find out how to categorize a contact, and then you see how to filter your Address Book list. Finally, you find out how to create new categories.

Categorize your contacts

Whether you're creating a contact or editing an existing contact, as long as you're in Edit mode, you can categorize that particular contact.

You can use these steps to add categories:

1. **From the Address Book, select a contact, press the Menu key, and then select Edit.**

2. **Press the Menu key and select Categories.**

   A Categories list appears. By default, you see only the Business and the Personal categories.

3. **Highlight Personal and press the SPACE key.**

4. **Press the Menu key and select Save.**

   You are brought back to the Edit screen for this particular contact.

5. **To complete your changes, press the Menu key and select Save (again).**

You now have one — count 'em, one — contact with Personal as its category, which means you can now filter your Address Book list using a category. Here's how:

1. **From the Address Book screen, press the Menu key and select Filter.**

   Your Categories list makes an appearance.

2. **Use the SPACE key or press the trackball to select the Personal check box.**

   Your Address Book list immediately shrinks to just the contacts assigned to the Personal category.

As you add more contacts to a category, you can also use Find and enter the first few letters of the name to search and further narrow the search for a contact. If you need a refresher on how this Find works, see the "Looking for Someone?" section, earlier in this chapter.

Adding a new category

Whoever thought the default categories (Business and Personal) were enough for the complexities of the real world probably didn't have many acquaintances, but that's neither here nor there. It's easy to add categories, so you can divide your world as much as you like. Just do the following:

1. **From the Address Book list screen, press the Menu key and select Filter.**

2. **Press the Menu key and select New.**

   A pop-up screen appears, asking you to name the new category you want to create.

3. **In the Name field, enter a name for your category and then press the trackball.**

   Your new category is saved. Now the Filter screen, which lists all the categories, includes the new one.

Applying a category filter

Having diligently assigned categories on your contacts, you can easily filter the Address Book list based on these categories. To do so, follow these steps:

1. **From the Address Book list screen, press the Menu key and select Filter.**

   The Categories screen appears.

2. **Highlight a Category and press the SPACE key.**

   Your Address Book list screen now shows the filtered contacts with the name of the Category as a header of the list.

You can remove the filter by repeating the process. When you get to the Categories screen, the Category you previously selected is marked by a check. By highlighting this Category and pressing the SPACE key, you're removing it as a filter.

You can quote me on this one

The purpose of groups is to easily scroll through your contacts, right? Assuming that you have a long list, your Family group could be buried in the middle of it — given where *F* falls in the alphabet. Or, you might not even remember one of the group names you used. (How embarrassing.) One simple technique to make a group appear at the very top of your contact list is to enclose it within single quotes. For example, instead of naming your group *Friends,* you could name it *'Friends.'* The single quote serves a double purpose:

✔ As a visual aid to quickly tell you that the contact listing is a group

✔ As a way to force groups to always list at the very top

Just make sure that none of your contact names are enclosed in single quotes.

Setting preferences

Sure there are some things you may want to behave differently in Address Book. The folks at RIM have anticipated some and made them available to you through Address Book *Options,* a palette of tricks you can use to navigate some out-of-the-ordinary situations. Here's the rundown:

✔ **Sort By:** Allows you to change the way the list is sorted. You can change the sort field criteria to First Name, Last Name, or Company. Use the SPACE key to toggle among the choices.

✔ **Confirm Delete:** Allows you to display a Confirmation screen for all contact deletions. You should always keep this feature turned on for normal usage. You could accidentally delete someone from your Address Book in many ways, so this feature is a good way of minimizing those accidents.

✔ **Allow Duplicate Names:** Self-explanatory. If you turn this on, you can have multiple people who happen to share the same name in your Address Book. If it's off, you get a warning when you try to add a name that's identical to someone who is already on your list. Maybe you are tired and are mistakenly trying to add the same person twice. Then again, sometimes people just have the same name. We recommend keeping the default value of Yes, allowing you to have contacts with the same names.

How do you change any of these options? The fields behave like any other fields in a BlackBerry application. You simply highlight the field, press the Menu key, and select Change Option from the menu that appears. You then see a menu screen that allows you to select the possible option values

Locating a Contact Using Maps

No, we don't mean finding someone in your Address Book. We literally mean finding where he or she is in the neighborhood. Your BlackBerry has a built-in Maps application. If you've used Google Maps on the Internet, you should be familiar with how this works.

You can access the Maps application by launching it using the Menu key from the Home screen. But what's neat is that it's seamlessly integrated with the Address Book. So if you have a contact and you put in a real address, you can highlight that contact from the Address Book screen and press the Menu key. You should see the menu item View Work Map or View Home Map or both, depending on which address is available, work or home. Selecting the option displays a map pointing to that specific address. Now, what you do with this map is up to you. You can use the trackball to position the map. Panning and zooming features are available through the Menu key.

One useful feature of the map is to get directions from location to location. While you're in the map, press the Menu key and select Directions. A screen appears, allowing you to enter from and to addresses. (If you open this map from Address Book, a list of addresses for the current contact are listed on this screen, so you can conveniently select from these addresses instead of entering one.) After entering from and to addresses, a screen appears, displaying a map and a listing of street-by-street turn directions. Try it.

Chapter 5

Never Miss Another Appointment

*T*o some folks, the key to being organized and productive is mastering time management and using their time wisely (and we're not just talking about reading this book while you're commuting to work). Many have discovered that there is no better way to organize one's time than to use a calendar — a daily planner tool. Some prefer digital to paper, so they use a planner software program on their PC — either installed on their hard drive or accessed through an Internet portal (such as Yahoo!). The smartest of the bunch, of course, use their BlackBerry Pearl handheld because it has the whole planner thing covered in handy form with its Calendar application.

In this chapter, we show you how to keep your life (personal and work) in order by managing your appointments with your BlackBerry Pearl Calendar. What's great about managing your time on a BlackBerry Pearl versus your PC is that your Pearl is always there with you to remind you. Just remember that you won't have excuses any more for forgetting that important quarterly meeting or Bertha's birthday bash.

Accessing the BlackBerry Pearl Calendar

The BlackBerry Pearl Calendar is one of the Pearl core applications, like Address Book or Phone (read more about the others in Chapter 1), so it's quite easy to get to. If you have the default BlackBerry Pearl theme named Zen, you can see the Calendar icon on the Home screen as one of the five applications on the bottom of your screen.

 To get cracking with your Calendar, from the Home screen, press the Menu key and select Calendar. Voilà! — you have Calendar.

Choosing Your Calendar View

The first time you open Calendar, you'll likely see the Day view, which is a default setting on the Pearl, as shown in Figure 5-1. You can change the Calendar view, however, to a different one that works better for your needs:

✔ **Day:** This view gives you a summary of your appointments for the day. By default, it lists all your appointments from 9 a.m. to 5 p.m.

✔ **Week:** This view shows you a seven-day summary view of your appointments. By using this view, you can see how busy you are for the week.

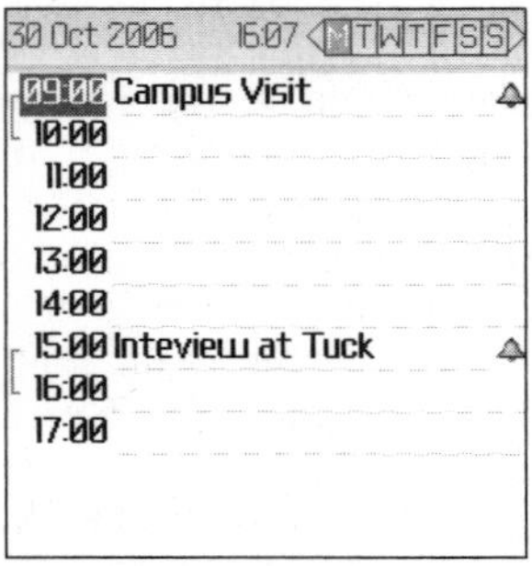

```
30 Oct 2006   16:07 ◁MTWTFSS▷
 09:00 Campus Visit          △
 10:00
 11:00
 12:00
 13:00
 14:00
 15:00 Inteview at Tuck      △
 16:00
 17:00
```

Figure 5-1: Day view in Calendar.

✔ **Month:** The Month view shows you every day of the month. You can't tell how many appointments are in a day, but you can see on which days you have appointments.

✔ **Agenda:** The Agenda view is a bit different from the other views. It isn't a time-based view like the others; it basically lists your upcoming appointments. And in the list, you can see details of the appointments, such as where and when.

Different views (like the ones shown in Figure 5-2) offer you a different focus on your schedule. Select the view you want based on your scheduling needs and preferences. If your life is a little more complicated, you can even use a combination of views for a full grasp of your schedule.

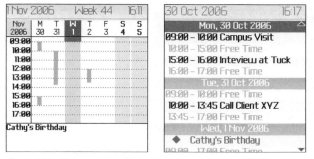

Figure 5-2: Change your Calendar view to fit your life.

To switch between different Calendar views, simply follow these steps:

1. **From the Home screen, press the Menu key and select Calendar.**

   Doing so calls up the Calendar application in its default view — more than likely the day view.

2. **Press the Menu key and select the view of your choice from the menu that appears (shown in Figure 5-3).**

   If you start from Day view, your choices are View Week, View Month, and View Agenda.

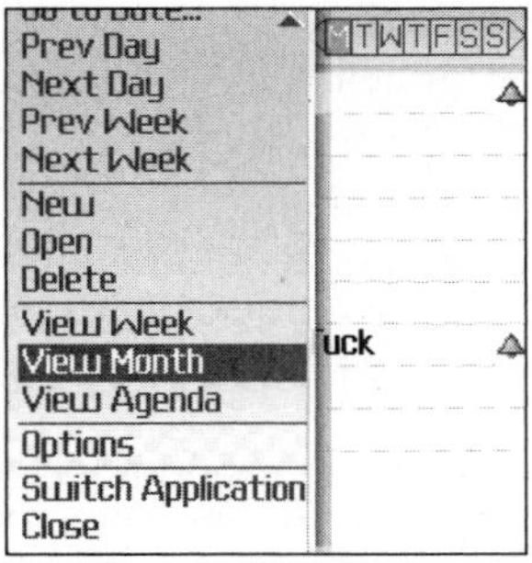

Figure 5-3: The Calendar menu lets you select different views.

Moving between Time Frames

Depending on what view of Calendar you're in, you can easily move to the previous or the next date, week, month, or year.

For example, if you're in the Month view, you can move to the next month (um, relative to the currently displayed month). Likewise, you can also move to the previous month. In fact, if you like to look at things long term, you can jump ahead (or back) a year at a time. (See Figure 5-4.)

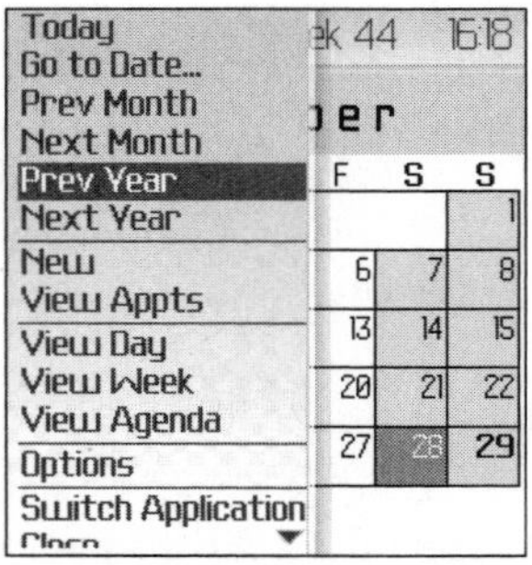

Figure 5-4: Move between months or years in Month view.

You have similar flexibility when it comes to the other Calendar views. See Table 5-1 for a summary of what's available.

Table 5-1	Moving between Views
Calendar View	*Move Between*
Day	Days and weeks
Week	Weeks
Month	Months and years
Agenda	Days

You can always go to today's date regardless of what Calendar view you're in. Just press the Menu key and select Today from the menu that appears.

Furthermore, you can jump to any date of your choosing by pressing the Menu key and selecting Go to Date from the menu that appears. Doing so calls up a handy little dialog box that lets you choose the date you want. To change the date, scroll the trackball to the desired day, month, and year, as shown in Figure 5-5.

Figure 5-5: Go to any date you want.

Customizing Your Calendar

To change the initial (default) view in your Calendar — from Day view to Month view, for example — Calendar Options is the answer.

To get to Calendar Options, open Calendar, press the Menu key, and select Options from the menu that appears. You see choices similar to the ones shown in Table 5-2.

Table 5-2	Calendar Options
Option	**Description**
Initial View	Specify the Calendar view that you first see when opening Calendar.
Enable Quick Entry	In Day view only, Quick Entry allows you to make a new appointment by typing characters. This way, you don't need to press the trackball and select New. *Note:* If you enable this, Day view shortcuts described on the cheat sheet (at the front of the book) would not apply.
Default Reminder	How long your BlackBerry Pearl notifies you before your appointment time. The default is 15 minutes.
Snooze	The snooze time when a reminder appears. The default is 5 minutes.
Start of Day	The time of day that defines your Start of Day in Day view. The default is 9 a.m. For example, if you change this to 8 a.m., your Day view starts at 8 a.m. instead of 9 a.m.
End of Day	The time of the day that defines End of Day in Day view. The default is 5 p.m. If you change this to 6 p.m., for example, your Day view ends at 6 p.m. instead of 5 p.m.
First Day of Week	The day that first appears in your Week view.
Confirm Delete	This option determines whether or not the Pearl prompts you for confirmation upon appointment deletion.
Show Free Time in Agenda View	If yes, this field allows an appointment-free day's date to appear in the Agenda view. If no, the Agenda view will not show the date of days on which you don't have an appointment.
Show End Time in Agenda View	If yes, this field shows the end time of each appointment in the Agenda view. If no, the Agenda view will show only the start time of each appointment.
Show Tasks	A task can be scheduled just like a Calendar event.
Number of Entries	The total number of appointments in your calendar (past and future).

All Things Appointments: Adding, Opening, and Deleting

After you master navigating the different Calendar views (and that should take you all of about two minutes), and you have Calendar customized to your heart's content (another three minutes, tops), it's time (pun intended) to set up, review, and delete appointments. We also show you how to set up a meeting with clients or colleagues.

Creating an appointment

Setting up a new appointment is easy. You need only one piece of information: when your appointment occurs. Of course, you can easily add related information about the appointment, such as the meeting's purpose, its location, and whatever additional notes are helpful.

 In addition to your standard one-time, limited-duration meeting, you can also set all-day appointments. The BlackBerry Pearl can assist you in setting recurring meetings as well as reminders. Sweet!

Creating a one-time appointment

To add a new, one-time appointment, follow these steps:

1. **Open Calendar.**

2. **Press the Menu key and select New.**

   The New Appointment screen appears, as shown in Figure 5-6.

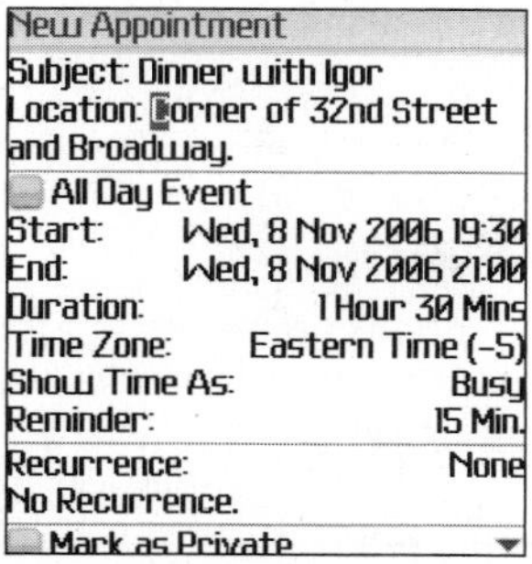

New Appointment
Subject: Dinner with Igor
Location: Corner of 32nd Street
and Broadway.
☐ All Day Event
Start: Wed, 8 Nov 2006 19:30
End: Wed, 8 Nov 2006 21:00
Duration: 1 Hour 30 Mins
Time Zone: Eastern Time (–5)
Show Time As: Busy
Reminder: 15 Min.
Recurrence: None
No Recurrence.
☐ Mark as Private

Figure 5-6: Set an appointment here.

3. **Fill in the key appointment information.**

    Type all the information regarding your appointment in the appropriate spaces. You should at least enter the time and the subject of your appointment.

4. **Press the Menu key and select Save.**

    This saves your newly created appointment.

Your new appointment is now in Calendar and viewable from any Calendar view. Also, keep in mind that you can have more than one appointment in the same time slot. Why? Well, the BlackBerry Pearl Calendar allows conflicts in your schedule because it lets you make the hard decision about which appointment you should forgo.

Creating an all-day appointment

If your appointment is an all-day event — for example, if you're in corporate training or have an all-day doctor's appointment — mark the All Day Event check box in the New Appointment screen, as shown in Figure 5-7. You can do so by scrolling to the check box and pressing the trackball. When this check box is checked, you will not be able to specify the time of your appointment — just the start date and end date (simply because it doesn't make sense to specify a time for an all-day event).

Appointment Details	
Subject: Freddie's bday	
Location:	
☑ All Day Event	
Start:	Sun, 29 Oct 2006
End:	Sun, 29 Oct 2006
Duration:	1 Day
Time Zone:	Eastern Time (–5)
Show Time As:	Free
Reminder:	15 Min.
Recurrence:	None
No Recurrence.	
☐ Mark as Private	
Notes:	▼

Figure 5-7: Set an all-day event here.

Setting your appointment reminder time

Any appointment you enter in Calendar can be associated with a reminder alert — either a vibration or a beep, depending on how you set things up in your profile. (For more on profiles, see Chapter 3.) You can also choose to have no reminder for an appointment. From the New Appointment screen, simply scroll to the Reminder field and select a reminder time anywhere from none to 1 week before your appointment time.

Profile is simply another useful BlackBerry Pearl feature that allows you to customize how your Pearl alerts you when an event occurs. Examples of events are an e-mail, a phone call, or a reminder for an appointment.

By default, whatever reminder alert you set goes off 15 minutes before the event. But you don't have to stick with the default. You can choose your own default reminder time. Here's how:

1. **Open Calendar.**

2. **Press the Menu key and select Options.**

   Doing so calls up the Calendar Options screen.

3. **Select Default Reminder.**

4. **Choose a default reminder time anywhere from none to 1 week before your appointment.**

So from now on, any new appointment has a default reminder time of what you just set up. Assuming that you have a reminder time other than none, the next time you have an appointment coming up, you see a dialog box like the one shown in Figure 5-8, reminding you of an upcoming appointment.

Figure 5-8: You get a reminder dialog box if you want.

Creating a recurring appointment

You can set up recurring appointments based on daily, weekly, monthly, or yearly recurrences. Everyone has some appointment that repeats, such as birthdays or anniversaries (or taking out the trash every Thursday at 7:30 a.m. — ugh).

For all recurrence types, you can define an Every field. For example, say you have an appointment that recurs every nine days. Just set the Recurrence field to Daily and the Every field to 9, as shown in Figure 5-9.

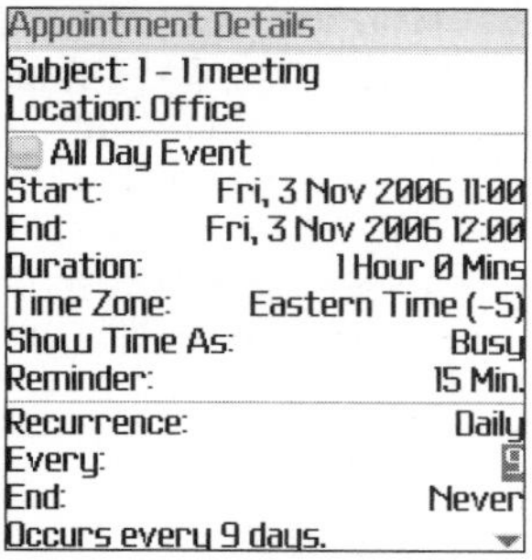

Figure 5-9: An appointment recurring every 9 days.

Depending on what you select in the Recurrence field, you have the option to fill in other fields. If you enter Weekly in the Recurrence field, for example, you have the option of filling in the Day of the Week field. (It basically allows you to select the day of the week on which your appointment recurs.)

If you enter Monthly or Yearly in the Recurrence field, the Relative Date check box is available. With this check box checked, you can ensure that your appointment recurs relative to today's date. For example, if you choose the following, your appointment occurs every two months on the third Sunday until July 31, 2010:

> **Start:** Sunday, June 18, 2006 at 12 p.m.
>
> **End:** Sunday, June 18, 2006 at 1 p.m.
>
> **Recurrence**: Monthly
>
> **Every**: 2
>
> **Relative Date**: Selected
>
> **End**: Saturday, July 31, 2010

On the other hand, if all options in our example remain the same except that Relative Date is not selected, your appointment occurs every two months, on the 18th of the month until July 31, 2010.

If all this "relative" talk has you dizzy, don't worry: The majority of your appointments won't be as complicated as this.

Opening an appointment

After you set an appointment, you can view it in a couple of ways. If you've set up reminders for your appointment and the little Reminder dialog box appears onscreen at the designated time before your appointment, you can view your appointment by clicking the box's Open button (refer to Figure 5-8). Or you can open the appointment from Calendar by going to the exact time of your appointment and viewing it there.

While looking at an appointment, you have the option of making changes (a new appointment time and new appointment location) and then saving them.

Deleting an appointment

Deleting an appointment is straightforward. When in Day or Week view, simply scroll to the appointment that you want to delete, press the Menu key, and select Delete from the menu that appears.

If the appointment that you're deleting is part of a recurring appointment, a dialog box pops up asking whether you want to delete all occurrences of this appointment or just this particular occurrence, as shown in Figure 5-10. After you make your choice, your appointment is history.

Figure 5-10: You can delete all occurrences or just the single instance of a recurring appointment.

Chapter 6

Making Notes and Keeping Your Words

....

In This Chapter

▶ Using MemoPad

▶ Managing your notes

▶ Keeping and retrieving your passwords

....

*Y*ou know what a memo pad is. Most people take them to meetings. Yes, you take them to those looong and sometimes boooring meetings. Bored and need to stay awake? Your memo pad is the answer. You can draw faces, doodle fanciful designs, or even write a poem, all the while pretending to listen to the blabbering of your colleagues or boss. What we describe in this chapter is your e-memo pad for taking notes — the aptly named MemoPad — on your BlackBerry. (Just no drawings faces, though.)

While we're on this note-taking business, we'll throw in the Password Keeper; a secure way of keeping your passwords in your BlackBerry.

MemoPad

MemoPad on your BlackBerry can prove handy, indeed. If nothing else, use it to jot important notes and ideas you might forget. How many frustrating times do we have to endure for not remembering a fleeting thought? We forget small things, and sometimes we forget important ones. Writing down your thoughts is the best solution. Or as you might expect from us, use your handy-dandy BlackBerry.

In upcoming sections, we explore how to jot down notes using MemoPad as well as how to effectively organize your notes and come back to them quickly using filters. And of course, more tips.

Accessing MemoPad

Accessing MemoPad is a snap. You can get to it using the Menu key from the Home screen. The left screen of Figure 6-1 shows the link to MemoPad from a T-Mobile Zen theme; a paper pad is the icon representing the application.

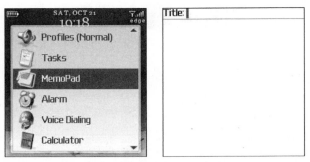

Figure 6-1: Open MemoPad here (left); start a new note here (right).

Jotting down notes

After you open MemoPad, recording notes is a breeze. Simply press the Menu key and select New. An empty memo screen appears, as shown on the right of Figure 6-1. A line divides the screen: The top field is for the title of your memo and the bottom part is where you enter your memo. There is no limit on the size of the memo as long as your BlackBerry has the capacity to store it.

When entering the note title, briefly describe the subject. If you use long words and a font size of 9, five words are about the optimum. The smaller the font, the more words you could fit on the screen.

You can enter more than six words — or as many as you want — but remember that the BlackBerry screen isn't wide. MemoPad displays the title as one line in the main MemoPad screen. If your note title is longer than the width of the screen, the title is truncated with an ellipsis (. . .) at its end.

Your MemoPad list is sorted alphabetically, so pay attention to choosing a helpful first word when entering the title. Use descriptive words and refrain from starting with *A*, *An*, *The*, *This*, and similar words.

Just like jotting down new memos, you can access all your memos easily in the MemoPad list and act on them using the menu.

Remember that the menu, just like in other applications, is always available by pressing the Menu key. The menu options that appear are in context with the currently selected memo, in this case giving you View, Edit, and Delete menu items.

Viewing your notes

Obviously, you jot a memo for future reference. Viewing the memo is the next logical step. After MemoPad is open, you can use the trackball to scroll and highlight the memo you want to view. Simply press the trackball and voila! A read-only screen displaying your memo shows up.

 If you're not happy with the font size, whether it's too small or too big, Chapter 3 has the details on how to customize display fonts. MemoPad is using the global preferences defined in Options (Screen/Keyboard).

View is the default action for a highlighted memo. By pressing the trackball, the highlighted memo displays in view or read-only mode.

Updating your notes

Change is inevitable. Or perhaps you made a mistake in your note taking. No problem. Updating your memo is easy. Just as when viewing your contact, highlight the memo you want to edit from the MemoPad list. Press the Menu key and select Edit. An editable screen similar to the screen you used to add a memo shows up. Make your edits and once you are contented, save them by pressing the Menu key and selecting Save.

Deleting your notes

Face it, half the sticky notes you find in your desk are no longer relevant. Your MemoPad is no different, so delete what you don't need. In your MemoPad list, highlight the memo you want to delete, and press the DEL key. The Delete Memo confirmation screen appears. Select Delete. Your memo is gone.

The confirmation screen you see when deleting a memo is a feature common to all out-of-the-box BlackBerry applications such as Address Book, Tasks, Calendar, and MemoPad. It diminishes the accidental deletion of records. You can enable or disable this feature. The ability to disable it is useful when you're dishing out lots of memos and don't want to be bothered with a confirmation screen for every memo to be deleted. (But then toggle the feature back on when you've finished deleting.)

To turn off this feature, do the following:

1. **In the MemoPad Options screen, highlight the Confirm Delete field.**

   The screen currently displays Yes. No means you want to toggle off the Confirmation screen.

2. **Press the SPACE key.**

   The MemoPad Options screen updates to show No in the Confirm Delete field.

3. **Press the Menu key and select Save.**

   The MemoPad application applies the changes you made.

Another field you can see from the MemoPad Options screen is Number of Entries. This field is just informational, showing you how many memos you have in your MemoPad application.

Quickly finding a note

When you open MemoPad, the first thing you'll see at the top of the screen is the Find field. You'll soon discover that this Find field is always present on the main MemoPad screen. Next to Find is an entry field. Just like the BlackBerry Address Book (see Chapter 4), you can use the Find feature to find a note. (Ah, the importance of good note naming becomes clearer all the time.)

Just start typing in the Find field, and the note list below shrinks based on matches. A match is simply a hit, based on the starting letters of *all* the words of the subjects in your list. As you type more letters in the Find field, your MemoPad note list is filtered more. For example, if you type **id**, Find filters the list for those notes with subjects having words that start with *id,* such as *ideas,* as you can see in Figure 6-2.

You may also organize your notes based on categories. Like in Address Book and Tasks, you can group your notes and then filter your note list based on a grouping. Simply define a group — a *category* — and then assign that category to a note. The steps are the same for Address Book, so refer to the "Using the Filter Feature on your contacts" section in Chapter 4 for a more detailed explanation of how categories work and how to apply them.

```
Find: id
Podcast Ideas
```

Figure 6-2: Search notes here.

The Password Keeper

With so many pins, user names, and passwords you have to remember these days, it's no wonder people tend to forget those that are not used frequently. How many times have you clicked the "Forget your id and password?" link on a Web site you've subscribed to? Don't head down to your local pharmacy for a memory enhancing drug; take that safe out of your pocket instead. That's right, among the many features of your BlackBerry, the ability to keep those passwords safe comes out of the box. We are talking here of the Password Keeper application. It's not only for passwords. You can store your other important information, such as your bank account numbers, your parent's social security number, anything.

Accessing Password Keeper

Yes, you can find Password Keeper by pressing the Menu key from the Home screen. Password Keeper is easy to spot because its icon looks like a big metal safe, as shown in Figure 6-3. (Figure 6-3 is taken from a T-Mobile Zen theme. Your Pearl will look different if you're using a different theme.)

Highlight the Password Keeper icon and press the trackball, and you are on your way to a spot that's more discrete than the Bat Cave.

Figure 6-3: Access Password Keeper here.

Setting a password for Password Keeper

The very first time you access Password Keeper, you're prompted to enter a password. *Please be sure to remember the password you choose* because this is the password to all your passwords. In addition, you are prompted to enter this master password every time you access Password Keeper.

We know it sounds perverse to set up yet another password to help you manage your passwords, but trust us. Having to remember just one password is a lot easier than having to remember 17.

Later, if you want to change your *master password* to Password Keeper — the password for opening Password Keeper itself — simply follow these steps:

1. **In the Home screen, press the Menu key and select Password Keeper.**

   The initial login screen for the Password Keeper application appears.

2. **Access Password Keeper by entering your old password.**

3. **With the Password Keeper application open, press the Menu key and select Change Password.**

   The Change Password screen appears, as shown in Figure 6-4.

4. **Enter a new password, confirm it, and then select OK.**

Figure 6-4: Change your Password Keeper password here.

Creating new credentials

Okay, so you're ready to fire up your handy dandy Password Keeper application. Now, what kinds of things does it expect you to do for it to work its magic? Obviously, you're going to need to collect the pertinent info for all your various password-protected accounts so that you can store them within the protected environs of Password Keeper. So, when creating a new password entry, be sure you have the following information (see the left screen of Figure 6-5):

- ✔ **Title:** This one's straightforward. Just come up with a name to describe the password-protected account — My Bank Account, for example.

- ✔ **Username:** This is where you enter the user name for the account.

- ✔ **Password:** Enter the password for the account here.

- ✔ **Website:** Put the Web site address (its URL) here.

- ✔ **Notes:** Not exactly crucial, but the Notes field gives you a bit of room to add a comment or two.

The only required field is Title, but a title alone usually isn't of much use. We suggest that you fill in as much other information here as possible, but at the same time *be discreet* about those locations where you use your user name and password — so don't put anything in the Website field or use My eBay Account as a title. That way, if someone *does* somehow gain access to your password to Password Keeper, the intruder will have a hard time figuring out where exactly to use your credentials.

```
New Password              New Password        ABC
Title:                    Title:
                          My Bank Password
Username:                 Username:

Password:                 Password:
                          >ekz_<0
Website:                  Website:
http://                   http://
Notes:                    Notes:
```

Figure 6-5: Set your new password here (left). A randomly generated password (right).

Random password generation

If you're the kind of person who uses one password for everything but knows deep in your heart that this is just plain wrong, wrong, wrong, Random Password generation is for you. It's quite simple. When creating a new password for yet another online account (or when changing your password for an online account you already have), fire up Password Keeper, press the Menu key, and then select Random Password from the menu that appears. Voilà! A new password is automatically generated, as shown in the right screen of Figure 6-5.

Using Random Password generation with Password Keeper makes sense because you don't have to remember the randomly generated password that Password Keeper came up with for any of your online accounts — that's Password Keeper's job.

Using your password

The whole point of Password Keeper is to let your BlackBerry's electronic brain do your password remembering for you. So, imagine this scenario: You can no longer live without owning a personal copy of the *A Chipmunk Christmas* CD, so you surf on over to your favorite online music store and attempt to log in. You draw a blank on your password, but instead of seething, you take out your BlackBerry, open the Password Keeper application, highlight the online site in your list, and press the trackball. The screen for your account appears, conveniently listing the password that was just on the tip of your tongue. All you have to do now is enter the password into the login screen for that online music store and Alvin,

Simon, and Theodore will soon be wending their way to your address, ready to sing "Chipmunk Jingle Bells."

Yes, you *do* have the option of copying and pasting your password from Password Keeper to another application — your BlackBerry Browser, for instance. Just highlight the password name, press the Menu key, and select Copy to Clipboard. Then navigate to where you want to enter the password, press the Menu key, and select Paste. Keep in mind that in order for the copy/paste function to work for passwords from Password Keeper, you need to enable the Allow Clipboard Copy option in the Password Keeper options (see the upcoming Table 6-1).

After you paste your password in another application, clear the Clipboard by pressing the Menu key and selecting Clear Clipboard. The Clipboard keeps your last copied password until you clear it.

You can copy and paste only one password at a time.

Password Keeper options

The Options screen allows you to control how Password Keeper behaves. For example, you can set what characters can make up a randomly generated password. See Table 6-1 for a listing of all options as well as descriptions of each one. To get to the Options screen, open Password Keeper, press the Menu key, and select Options.

Table 6-1	Password Keeper Options
Option	*Description*
Random Password Length	Select between 4 and 16 for the length of your randomly generated password.
Random Includes Alpha	If True, a randomly generated password includes alphabetic characters.
Random Includes Numbers	If True, a randomly generated password includes numbers.
Random Includes Symbols	If True, a randomly generated password includes symbols.
Confirm Delete	If True, all deletions are prompted with a Confirmation screen.

(continued)

Table 6-1 *(continued)*

Option	Description
Password Attempts	Select between 1 and 20 attempts to successfully enter the password to Password Keeper.
Allow Clipboard Copy	If True, you can copy and paste passwords from Password Keeper.
Show Password	If True, the password appears in the View screen. If False, asterisks take the place of password characters.

Part III
Getting Multimedia and Going Online with Your Pearl

The 5th Wave   By Rich Tennant

In this part . . .

*H*ere's the good stuff —md using your BlackBerry for e-mail (Chapter 7), text messaging (Chapter 8), going online and Web surfing (Chapter 9), and making those all-important phone calls (Chapter 10). Prepare to take pictures using the camera (Chapter 11) and set your mood listening to music and watching video clips (Chapter 12).

Chapter 7

You've Got (Lots of) E-Mail

*Y*our BlackBerry Pearl brings a fresh new face to the convenience and ease-of-use that we associate with e-mail. You can direct mail to your Pearl from up to ten e-mail accounts from the likes of AOL and Yahoo!. You can set up an e-mail signature, configure e-mail filters, and search for e-mails.

In this chapter, we show you how to use and manage the mail capabilities of your Pearl to their full potential. From setup to sorts, we've got you covered here.

Getting Up and Running with E-Mail

Regardless of your network service provider (such as T-Mobile or Rogers or Vodafone), you can set up your BlackBerry Pearl to receive mail from at least one of your current e-mail accounts. Thus, with whatever address you use to send and receive e-mail from your PC (Yahoo!, Gmail, and so on), you can hook up your Pearl to use that same e-mail address. Instead of checking your Gmail at the Google site, for example, you can now get it on your BlackBerry Pearl.

 Most network service providers allow you to connect up to ten e-mail accounts to your BlackBerry. This provides you with the convenience of one central point from which you get all your e-mail, without having to log into multiple e-mail accounts. Such convenience!

Using the BlackBerry Internet Service client

You can pull together all your e-mail accounts into one by using the *BlackBerry Internet Service client* (former known as BlackBerry Web client). The BlackBerry Internet Service client allows you to

- ✔ **Manage up to ten e-mail accounts:** You can combine up to ten of your e-mail accounts onto your BlackBerry. See the upcoming section, "Combining your e-mail accounts into one."

- ✔ **Use wireless e-mail reconciliation:** No more trying to match your BlackBerry e-mail against e-mail in your combined account(s). Just turn on wireless e-mail reconciliation and you're good to go. For more on this, see the upcoming section, "Enabling wireless reconciliation."

- ✔ **Create e-mail filters:** You can filter e-mails so that you get only those e-mail messages that you truly care about on your BlackBerry. See the section "Filtering your e-mail" near the end of this chapter.

Think of the BlackBerry Internet Service client (Service client) as an online e-mail account manager. Unlike other online e-mail accounts, Service client doesn't keep your e-mails. Instead, it routes the e-mails from your other accounts to your BlackBerry Pearl (because it's directly connected to your Pearl).

Combining your e-mail accounts into one

To start aggregating e-mail accounts (like Gmail) onto your Pearl, you must first run a setup program from the BlackBerry Internet Service client. You can access the Service client from your BlackBerry Pearl or from your desktop computer.

To access the Service client from your PC, you need the URL that is specific to your network service. Contact your network service provider for the URL and login information.

After you've logged into the Service client, you should see something similar to Figure 7-1. If your BlackBerry Pearl has been activated by your network provider, you should see one e-mail address, the default address of your BlackBerry Pearl.

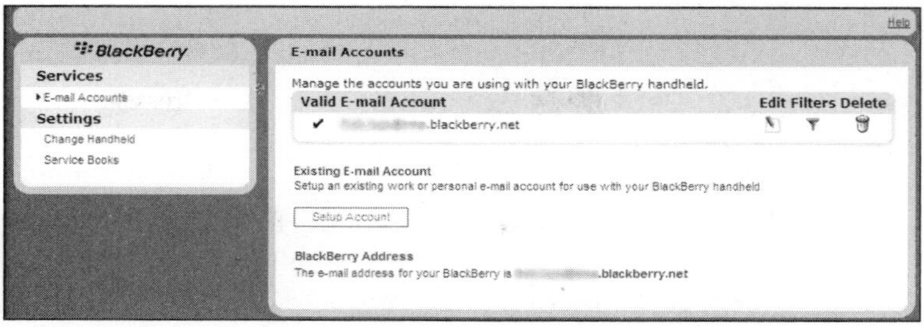

Figure 7-1: Set up an e-mail account here.

From the Service client, you should see three options on the left navigation bar:

- ✔ **E-mail Accounts:** Here, you can add, edit, and delete e-mail accounts. In addition, for each e-mail address, you can set up filters and an e-mail signature.

- ✔ **Change Handheld:** This option isn't used frequently, and we won't be covering it here.

- ✔ **Service Books:** This option isn't used frequently, and we won't be covering it here.

As mentioned, your BlackBerry Pearl already has a default e-mail address with which you can receive and send e-mail. If you don't have any other e-mail account that you want to meld into your BlackBerry e-mail account, simply skip to the upcoming "Configuring your e-mail signature" section.

Adding an e-mail account

You can have up to ten e-mail accounts on your BlackBerry — this is the good stuff right here. To add an e-mail account to your BlackBerry account, follow these steps:

1. **From the BlackBerry Internet Service client (refer to Figure 7-1), click the Setup Account button.**

   You see the Add e-mail account screen.

2. **From the Add e-mail account screen, enter the e-mail address and login credentials for that e-mail address.**

   - The e-mail address is the address from which you want to receive e-mail: for example, myid@yahoo.com.

   - The account login is the one you use to log into this particular e-mail account.

- The password is the one you use associated with the login.

3. **Click the Next button.**

    You're finished. It's that easy!

You can also manage your accounts from your BlackBerry Pearl. From the Home screen, press the Menu key and select Set up Internet E-mail. The rest is pretty much the same on the BlackBerry as it is on a PC.

Configuring your e-mail signature

By default, your e-mail signature is something like "Sent via My BlackBerry" which can be cool in the first week, showing off to people that you are a la mode with your BlackBerry Pearl. But sooner or later, you might not want people to know you are out and about while answering e-mail. Or you might want something more personal. Follow these steps to configure your e-mail signature using the Service client:

1. **Log into the Service client.**

2. **From the BlackBerry Internet Service client (refer to Figure 7-1), click the Edit icon for the desired e-mail account.**

    The edit screen appears, as show in Figure 7-2.

3. **In the Signature field, type the desired text for your e-mail signature.**

4. **Click Save.**

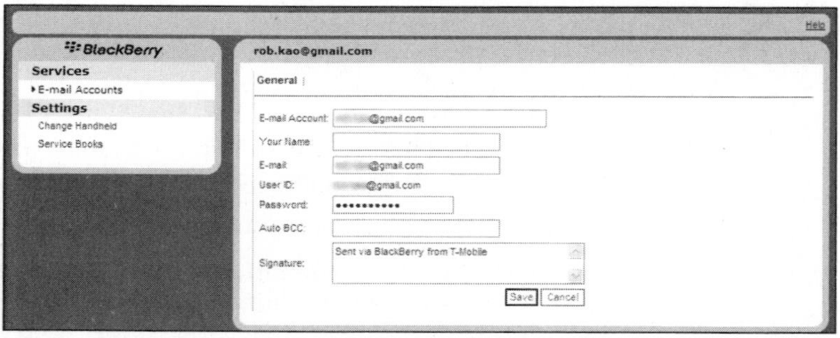

Figure 7-2: Showing the e-mail account edit screen.

Enabling wireless reconciliation

With wireless reconciliation, you don't need to delete the same e-mail in two places: The two e-mail in boxes reconcile with each other, hence the term *wireless reconciliation*. Convenient, huh?

Enabling wireless e-mail synchronization

You can start wireless e-mail synchronization by configuring your BlackBerry:

1. **From the Home screen, press the Menu Key and select Messages.**

   This opens the Messages application. You see the message list.

2. **In the message list, press the Menu key and select Options.**

   The Options screen appears, with two option types: General Options and Email Reconciliation.

3. **Select Email Reconciliation.**

   This opens the Email Reconciliation screen, which has the following options:

   - *Delete On:* This option configures how BlackBerry handles your e-mail deletion.

   - *Wireless Reconciliation:* This option turns on or off the wireless sync function.

   - *On Conflict:* This option controls how BlackBerry handles inconsistency between e-mail on your BlackBerry versus BlackBerry Internet Service client.

     You can choose who "wins" via this option: your BlackBerry or the BlackBerry Internet Service client.

4. **Select Delete On, and then select one of the following from the drop-down list:**

   - *Handheld:* A delete on your BlackBerry takes effect on your BlackBerry only.

   - *Mailbox & Handheld:* A delete on your BlackBerry takes effect on both your BlackBerry and your inbox on BlackBerry Internet Service client.

   - *Prompt:* This option prompts your BlackBerry to ask you at the time of deletion.

5. **Select Wireless Reconciliation, and then select On from the drop-down list.**

6. **Select On Conflict, and make a selection from the drop-down list.**

   If you choose Handheld Wins, the e-mail in your e-mail account will match the ones on the handheld.

Unfortunately, some e-mail accounts might not work well with the e-mail reconciliation feature of the BlackBerry Pearl. So you might have to delete an e-mail twice.

Permanently deleting e-mail from your BlackBerry

When deleting e-mail on your BlackBerry, the same message in that e-mail account is placed in the Deleted folder. You can set up your BlackBerry to permanently delete e-mail, but use this option with caution — after that e-mail is gone, it's gone.

To permanently delete e-mail on your Service client from your BlackBerry, follow these steps:

1. **Open the Messages application.**

2. **In the message list, press the Menu key and select Options.**

3. **In the Options screen, select Email Reconciliation.**

4. **In the Email Reconciliation screen, press the Menu key and select Purge Deleted Items.**

   A pop-up appears listing all your e-mail accounts.

5. **From the pop-up menu, choose the e-mail account from which you want to purge deleted items.**

   Another pop-up appears confirming that you are about to purge deleted e-mails on your Service client.

6. **Select Yes.**

   Deleted e-mails in the selected e-mail account are purged.

Unfortunately, some e-mail accounts might not work with the purge deleted items feature.

Accessing Messages

From Messages, you send and receive your e-mails and also configure wireless e-mail reconciliation with your e-mail account(s).

To access Messages, from the Home screen, press the Menu key and select Messages. The first thing you see after opening Messages is the message list. Your message list can contain e-mail, voice mail messages, missed phone call notices, Short Messaging Service (SMS) messages, and even saved Web pages.

Receiving e-mails

Whether you're concerned about security or speed of delivery, with BlackBerry Pearl's up-to-date secured network, you're in good hands when receiving e-mail on your BlackBerry Pearl.

And whether you've aggregated accounts or just use the plain-vanilla BlackBerry Pearl e-mail account, you receive your e-mail the same way. When you receive an e-mail, your BlackBerry Pearl notifies you by displaying a numeral next to a mail icon (an enve-lope) at the top of the screen. This number represents how many new (unread) e-mails you have. See Figure 7-3. The asterisk next to the envelope indicates that there is new mail and you haven't opened the Messages application yet.

Your BlackBerry Pearl can also notify you of new e-mail by vibra-tion or a sound alert or both. You can customize this from Profile, as we detail in Chapter 3.

Figure 7-3: You've got (3) e-mails!

Retrieving e-mail

Retrieving your e-mail is simple:

1. **From the Home screen, press the Menu key and select Messages.**

   Doing so allows you to view your message list.

2. **In the message list, scroll to any e-mail and press the trackball.**

You can tell whether an e-mail is unopened by the small unopened envelope icon on the left side of the e-mail. A read e-mail bears an opened envelope icon, a sent e-mail has a check mark as its icon, and a draft e-mail is represented by a document icon.

3. **After you finish reading the message, press the Escape key to return to the message list.**

Saving a message to the saved folder

You can save any important e-mail into a folder so you can find it without sorting through tons of e-mail. To do so, simply scroll to the e-mail you want to save, press the Menu key, and select Save from the menu. A pop-up message confirms that your e-mail has been saved. *Note:* Your saved e-mail still remains in the message list.

To retrieve or view a saved e-mail, follow these steps:

1. **Open the Messages application.**

2. **In the message list, press the Menu key and select View Saved Messages.**

You see the list of all the messages you saved.

3. **Select the message you want and press the trackball to open it.**

Viewing attachments

Your BlackBerry Pearl is so versatile that you can view most e-mail attachments just like you can on a desktop PC. And we're talking sizeable attachments, too, such as JPEGs (photos), Word docs, PowerPoint slides, and Excel spreadsheets. Table 7-1 has a list of supported attachment viewable from your BlackBerry Pearl.

Table 7-1	BlackBerry Pearl-Supported Attachments
Supported Attachment Extension	*Description*
`.zip`	Compressed file format
`.htm`	HTML Web page
`.html`	HTML Web page

Supported Attachment Extension	Description
.doc	MS Word document
.dot	MS Word document template
.ppt	MS PowerPoint document
.pdf	Adobe PDF document
.wpd	Corel WordPerfect document
.txt	Text file
.xls	MS Excel document
.bmp	BMP image file format
.gif	GIF image file format
.jpg	JPEG image file format
.png	PNG image file format
.tif	TIFF image file format

However versatile your BlackBerry Pearl is, you can't create certain types of attachments (MS Word, Excel, PDF) without help from third-party software. Please refer to Chapter 17 for a productivity program that can help you create Word docs and Excel spreadsheets right from your BlackBerry Pearl and attach them in an e-mail for you to send. However, you can attach pictures that are stored on your BlackBerry Pearl. See Chapter 11 for details.

To tell whether an e-mail has an attachment, look for the standard paperclip icon next to your e-mail in the message list.

You retrieve all the different types of attachments the same way. This makes retrieving attachments an easy task. To open an attachment, follow along:

1. **While reading an e-mail, press the Menu key and select Open Attachment.**

   You see a screen containing the name of the file, a Table of Contents option, and a Full Contents option. For MS Word documents, you can see different headings in outline form in the Table of Contents option. For picture files, such as a JPEG, you can simply go straight to the Full Contents option to see the graphic.

For all supported file types, you see Table of Contents and Full Contents as options. Depending on the file type, use your judgment on when you should use the Table of Contents option.

2. **Scroll to Full Contents, press the Menu key, and select Retrieve.**

   Your BlackBerry Pearl attempts to contact the BlackBerry server to retrieve your attachment. This retrieves only part of your attachment. As you peruse a document, BlackBerry Pearl retrieves more as you scroll through the attachment. When you're retrieving a picture, all parts of the attachment will appear.

Sending e-mail

The first thing you probably want to do when you get your BlackBerry Pearl is to write an e-mail to let your friends know that you've just gotten a BlackBerry Pearl. Follow these steps:

1. **Open the Messages application. In the message list, press the Menu key and select Compose Email.**

   You are prompted with a blank e-mail that you just need to fill out as you would do on you PC.

2. **In the To field, type your recipient's name or e-mail address.**

   As you type, you'll see a list of contacts from your Address Book matching the name or address that you're typing.

3. **Type your message subject and body.**

4. **When you're finished, press the Menu key and select Send.**

   Your message has wings.

Forwarding e-mail

When you need to share an important e-mail with a colleague or a friend, you can forward that e-mail. Simply do the following:

1. **Open the e-mail.**

   For information on opening e-mail, see the previous section, "Retrieving e-mail."

2. **Press the Menu key and select Forward.**

3. **Type the recipient's name or e-mail address in the appropriate space, then add a message if needed.**

   When you start typing your recipient's name, a drop-down list of your contacts will appear and you can choose from it.

4. **Press the Menu key and select Send.**

   Your message is on its way to your recipient.

Saving a draft e-mail

Sometimes the most skillful wordsmiths find themselves lost for words to express the message they want. Don't fret, fellow wordsmith, you can save that e-mail composition as a draft until your words come back to you. You only need to press the Menu key and select Save Draft.

This saves your e-mail as a draft. When you're ready to send your message, choose the draft from the message list. You can tell which messages are drafts because they sport a tiny Document icon; finished messages have an envelope icon.

Adding a sender to your Address Book

You can add a message-sender's contact info to your BlackBerry Pearl Address Book directly from Messages. You don't even have to copy or write down the person's name and e-mail address on paper.

To add a sender to your Address Book, follow these steps:

1. **From the Home screen, press the Menu key and select Messages.**

2. **In the message list, scroll to an e-mail and press the trackball.**

3. **From the open e-mail, scroll to the sender's name, press the trackball, and then choose Add to Address Book.**

   The New Address screen opens. The sender's first name, last name, and e-mail address are automatically transferred to your Address Book.

4. **If needed, add any additional information (such as a phone number and a mailing address).**

5. **Press the Menu key and select Save.**

Filtering your e-mail

Most of us get e-mail that either isn't urgent or doesn't really concern us. Instead of receiving them on your BlackBerry Pearl — and wasting both time and effort to check them — you can filter them out. While in the BlackBerry Pearl Internet Service client, set up filters to make your BlackBerry Pearl mailbox receive only those e-mails that you care about. (Don't worry; you'll still receive them on your main computer.)

We'll create a simple filter that treats work-related messages as urgent and forwards them to your BlackBerry Pearl. Follow these steps:

1. **Log into the BlackBerry Internet Service client (refer to Figure 7-1).**

2. **Click the Filter icon for the desired e-mail account.**

   The Filter screen that appears shows a list of filters that have been created. See Figure 7-4.

Figure 7-4: Filter list screen.

3. **Click the Click here link.**

   The Add Filter screen appears, as shown in Figure 7-5.

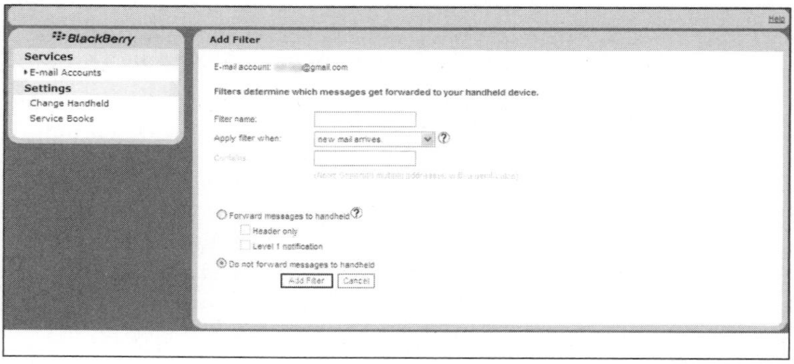

Figure 7-5: Create a filter for your e-mail here.

4. **Enter a filter name.**

   The filter name can be anything you like. We entered **WorkUrgent**.

5. **In the Apply Filter When drop-down list, choose the condition to place on the filter:**

   - *A high-priority mail arrives:* Select this option if the filter applies only to urgent e-mail.

   - *Subject field contains:* When selected, the Contains field is enabled (you can type text into it). You can specify what keywords the filter will look for in the subject field. Separate each entry with a semicolon (;).

   - *From field contains:* When selected, the Contains field is enabled (you can type text into it). You can type in full addresses or part of an address. For example, you can type *rob@robkao.com* or just *kao*. Separate each entry with a semicolon (;).

   - *To field contains:* Works similar to From field contains.

   - *CC field contains:* Works similar to From field contains.

     To follow along with us, select From field contains.

6. **Specify the text in the Contains field.**

   See details in the preceding step for what to enter in the Contains field. Continuing our example, type the domain of your work e-mail address. For example, if your work e-mail address is myName@XYZCo.com, enter **XYZCo.com**.

7. **Select one of the following options:**

   Forward Messages to Handheld: You can select either or both of the following two check boxes:

   - *Header Only:* Choose this if you want only the header of the e-mails that meet the condition(s) you set in Steps 3, 4, and 5 to be sent to you. (A *header* doesn't contain the body of the e-mail — just who sent it, the subject, and the time it was sent.) You would choose this if you get automated alerts, where receiving only the subject is sufficient.

   - *Level 1 Notification:* Level1 notification is another way of saying *urgent e-mail*. When you receive a Level1 e-mail, it is bold in Messages.

   Do Not Forward Message to Handheld: Selecting this means that any e-mail that meets the conditions you set in Steps 3, 4, and 5 will not be sent to your BlackBerry Pearl.

8. Confirm your filter by clicking the Add Filter button.

You return to the Filter screen, where you can see your newly created filter in the list.

If you have a hard time setting the criteria for a filter, just take a best guess and then test it by having a friend send you a test e-mail. If the test e-mail didn't get filtered correctly, set the conditions until you get them right.

Searching through Your Messages Like a Pro

Searching is one of those functions you probably won't use every day — but when you do run a search, you usually need the information fast. Take a few minutes here to familiarize yourself with the general search.

Running a general search

A general search is a broad search from which you can perform keyword searches of your messages.

To run a general search:

1. Open the Messages application.

2. In the messages list, press the Menu key and select Search.

3. In the Search screen that appears, fill in your search criteria (see Figure 7-6).

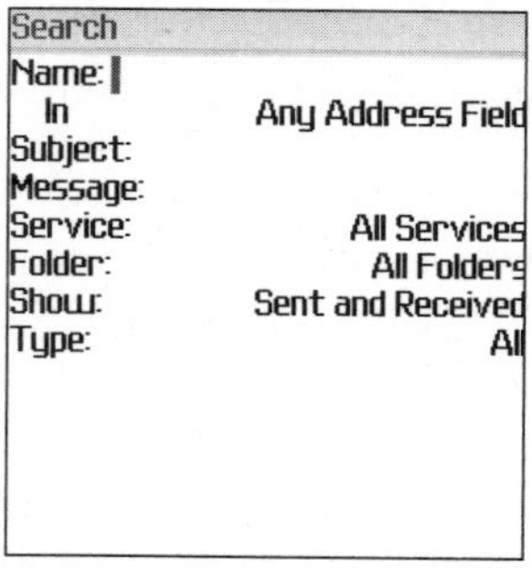

```
Search
Name:│
  In            Any Address Field
Subject:
Message:
Service:        All Services
Folder:         All Folders
Show:       Sent and Received
Type:                     All
```

Figure 7-6: The Search screen in Messages.

The search criteria for a general search follow:

- *Name:* This is the name of the sender or recipient to search by.

- *In Field:* This is related to the Name criterion. Use this drop-down list to indicate where the name might appear, such as in the To or Cc field. Your choices are the From, To, Cc, Bcc, or any address fields.

- *Subject:* This is where you type some or all the key-words that appear in the subject.

- *Message:* Here you enter keywords that appear in the message.

- *Service:* If you set up your Pearl to receive e-mail from more than one e-mail account, you can specify which e-mail account to search for.

- *Folder:* This is the folder in which you want to per-form the search. Generally, you should search all folders.

- *Show:* This drop-down list specifies how the search result will appear: namely, whether you want to see only e-mails that you sent or e-mails that you received. From the drop-down list, your choices are Send and Received, Received Only, Sent Only, Saved Only, Draft Only, and Unopened Only.

- *Type:* This drop-down list specifies the type of mes-sage that you're trying to search for: e-mail, SMS, or voice mail. From the drop-down list, your choices are: All, Email, Email With Attachments, PIN, SMS, Phone, Voice Mail.

From the Search screen shown in Figure 7-6, you can have multiple search criteria or just a single one (up to you).

 4. Press the Menu key and select Search to launch your search.

The search results appear onscreen.

You can narrow the search results by performing a second search on the initial results. For example, you can search by sender and then narrow those hits by performing a second search by subject.

You can search by subject when you're looking for a specific e-mail titled by a specific subject that you already know. Just scroll to an e-mail bearing the same specific subject you're searching for, press the Menu key, and select Search Subject.

You can also search by sender or recipient when you're looking for a specific message from a specific person. To do so, scroll to an e-mail bearing the specific sender or recipient. Press the Menu key and select Search Sender or Search Recipient. If the e-mail that you highlighted is an incoming e-mail, you'll see Search Sender. On the other hand, if the e-mail is outgoing, you'll see Search Recipient.

Saving search results

If you find yourself re-searching by using the same criteria over and over, you might want to save the search and then reuse it. Here's how:

1. **Follow Steps 1 through 3 in the "Running a general search" section for an outgoing e-mail search.**

2. **Press the Menu key and select Save.**

   The Search Save screen appears, from which you can name your search and assign it a shortcut key. See Figure 7-7.

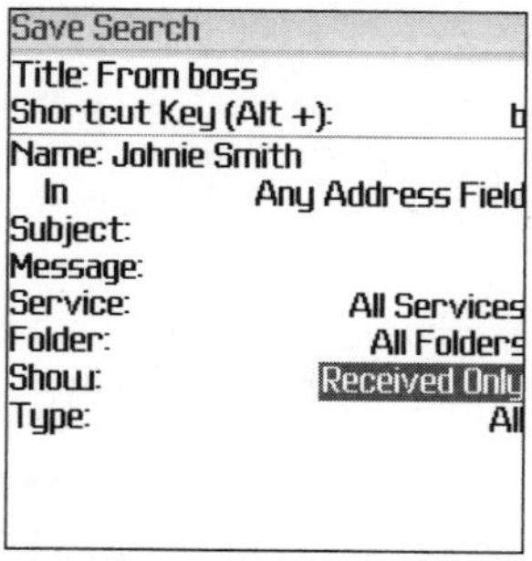

Figure 7-7: Name your search and assign a shortcut key.

3. **In the Title field, enter a name.**

   The title is the name of your search, which appears in the Search Result screen.

4. **Scroll to Shortcut Key field, press the trackball, and select a letter from the drop-down list.**

   You have ten letters to choose from.

5. **Confirm your saved search by pressing the Menu key and selecting Save.**

Reusing saved search results

Right out of the box, your BlackBerry Pearl comes with five saved search results. Any new saved result will make your search that much more robust.

To see all the saved search results:

1. **Open the Messages application.**

2. **In the message list, press the Menu key and select Search.**

3. **Press the Menu key and select Recall.**

   The recall screen opens, and you can see the five pre-loaded search shortcuts, as shown in Figure 7-8.

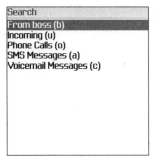

Figure 7-8: The recall screen, showing default search hot keys.

To reuse one of saved search results, simply select a desired search from list in Figure 7-8, press the Menu key, and select Search.

Long Live E-Mail

No closet has unlimited space, and your BlackBerry Pearl e-mail storage has limits, too. You've likely pondered how long your e-mails are kept in your BlackBerry Pearl. (The default is 30 days. Pshew.) You can choose several options: from 15 days to forever (well, for as long as your BlackBerry Pearl has enough space for them).

Because any message you save is kept for as long as you want, a good way to make sure you don't lose an important message is to save it.

To change how long your e-mails live on your BlackBerry Pearl, follow these steps:

1. **Open Messages application.**

2. **Press the Menu key and select Options.**

3. **Select General Options.**

4. **Scroll to the Keep Messages option and press the trackball.**

5. **From the drop-down list that appears, choose the time frame that you want and then press the trackball.**

   • *Forever:* If you choose Forever, you'll seldom need to worry about your e-mails being automatically deleted. On the downside, though, you'll eventually run out of memory on your BlackBerry Pearl. At that point, you must manually delete some e-mail so that you have space to accept new e-mail.

   A good way to archive your e-mail is to back up your e-mails using BlackBerry Desktop Manager. See Chapter 14 for more on backing up your Pearl on your PC.

   • *Time option:* If you choose a set-time option, any message older than that time frame is automatically deleted from your BlackBerry Pearl the next time you reboot your Pearl. However, it will be deleted only on your Pearl — even if you turn on e-mail reconciliation — because these deletions are not completed manually by you.

6. **Confirm your changes by pressing the Menu key and selecting Save.**

Chapter 8

Too Cool for E-Mail

*Y*our BlackBerry is primarily a communication tool, with e-mail messages and phone conversations being the major drivers here. The social creatures that people are, however, we constantly come up with new ways to communicate — ever more ways to overcome the distance barrier, as it were. You shouldn't be surprised that the folks at RIM have moved beyond e-mail and phoning in their search for other ways to communicate. (And we're not talking semaphore or stringing together two tin cups.)

Not that we're dismissing the power of phones or e-mail. Both are wonderful technologies, but you might find yourself in a situation where other means of communication would be more appropriate. For instance, for instant messaging or chatting, e-mail is too slow and cumbersome. Nor is e-mail really the best tool to use when you want to alert someone.

"What might be a better fit?" you ask. Read this chapter to find out. You can familiarize yourself with some of the less obvious ways you can use your BlackBerry to communicate — ways that might serve as the perfect fit for a special situation. You'll get the inside scoop on PIN-to-PIN messaging and text messaging (also known as Short Messaging Service, or SMS). We also give you tips on how to turn your BlackBerry into a lean (and not so mean) instant messaging machine.

Sending and Receiving PIN-to-PIN Messages

What actually happens when you use PIN-to-PIN messaging? First and foremost, get the acronym out of the way. *PIN* stands for personal identification number (familiar to anyone who's ever used an ATM) and refers to a system for uniquely identifying your device. *PIN-to-PIN,* then, is another way of saying *One BlackBerry to another BlackBerry.*

As for the other details, they're straightforward. PIN-to-PIN messaging is based on the technology underpinning two-way pager systems, which is fast. When you send a PIN-to-PIN message, unlike a standard e-mail message, the message doesn't venture outside RIM's infrastructure in search of an e-mail server and (eventually) an e-mail inbox. Instead, the message stays solidly within the RIM world, where it is shunted through the recipient's network provider until it ends up on the recipient's BlackBerry. Trust us when we say it's fast. You have to try it to see the difference.

Getting a BlackBerry PIN

When you try to call somebody on the telephone, you can't get far without a telephone number. As you might expect, the same principle applies to PIN-to-PIN messaging: No PIN, no PIN-to-PIN messaging. In practical terms, this means you need the individual PIN of any BlackBerry device owned by whomever you want to send a PIN message to. (You also need to find out your own PIN so you can hand it out to those folks who want to PIN-message you.) The cautious side of you might be thinking, "Now, why on earth would I give my PIN to somebody?" This PIN is really not the same as your password. In fact, this PIN doesn't give anybody access to your BlackBerry or do anything to compromise security. It's simply an identification; you treat it the same way as you treat your phone number.

RIM makes getting hold of a PIN easy. In fact, RIM even provides you with multiple paths to PIN enlightenment, as the following list makes clear:

  ✔ **From the Message screen:** RIM makes it easy for you to send your PIN from the Message screen with the help of a keyword. A *keyword* is a neat feature with which you type a preset word, and your BlackBerry replaces what you type with a bit of information specific to your device.

It's easier than it sounds. To see what we mean, just compose a new e-mail in the Message application. In the subject or body of your message, type **mypin** and add a space. As soon as you type the space, mypin is miraculously transformed into your PIN in the format pin:*your-pin-number*. Isn't that neat?

mypin isn't the only keyword that RIM predefines for you.

✔ **From the Status screen:** You can find your PIN also on the Status screen. From the Home screen, press the Menu key, select Options, and then select Status to display the Status screen.

Assigning PINs to names

So, you convince your BlackBerry-wielding buddies to go to the trouble of finding out their PINs and passing said PINs to you. Now, the trick is finding a convenient place to store your PINs so you can use them. Luckily for you, you have an obvious choice: BlackBerry Address Book. PIN is a contact field in Address Book. Refer to the "Editing a Contact" section in Chapter 4 for getting that PIN information into your buddies' contact record.

Sending a PIN-to-PIN message

Sending a PIN-to-PIN message is no different than sending an e-mail. Here's how:

1. **From the Home screen, press the Menu key and select Address Book.**

   The Address Book opens.

2. **Highlight a contact name, press the Menu key, and select PIN *<contact name>*.**

   Say, for example, that you have a contact named *Dante Sarigumba.* When you highlight Dante Sarigumba in the list and press the Menu key, the menu item *PIN Dante Sarigumba* appears as an option.

3. **Press Enter.**

   The ever-familiar New Message screen, with the PIN of your buddy already entered as an address, makes an appearance. Treat the other e-mail-creation stuff — adding a subject line, entering the body of your message, and then signing off — just as you would with a normal e-mail.

Because of the nature of PIN-to-PIN messaging (the conspicuous lack of a paper trail, as it were), RIM has set it up so that companies can disable PIN-to-PIN messaging on your BlackBerry device. (No paper trail can mean legal problems down the road — can you say *Sarbanes-Oxley*?) If your BlackBerry Pearl is from your employer and you don't see the PIN menu item allowing you to send PIN-to-PIN messages, you can safely assume that your employer has disabled it. Contact your company's BlackBerry administrator to make sure. Keep in mind that even if your company has disabled PIN-to-PIN messaging, folks can still PIN you — you just won't be able to PIN them back in response.

Receiving a PIN-to-PIN message

Receiving a PIN-to-PIN message is no different than receiving a standard e-mail. You get the same entry into your Messages list for the PIN-to-PIN message that you receive, and the same message screen displays when you open the message. By default, your BlackBerry vibrates to alert you, but this behavior can be customized in Profiles. In Profiles, PIN-to-PIN is a Level1 message. (Check Chapter 3 for details on changing your Profile.) When you reply to the message, the reply is a PIN-to-PIN message as well — that is, as long as your BlackBerry is set up to send PIN-to-PIN messages.

Keeping in Touch, the SMS/MMS Way

Short Messaging Service (also known as *SMS*, or simply *text messaging*) is so popular these days that even the Fox Network TV show *American Idol* lets you vote for the show's contestants through SMS. Moreover, SMS is an established technology (not a new and unproven thing, in other words) that has been popular for years in Europe and Asia, where the Global System for Mobile Communication (GSM) is the technology of choice among cellphone network providers. How short is short? The maximum size per message is about 160 characters. If you send more than that, your message gets broken down into multiple messages.

Multimedia Messaging Service (*MMS*) is the latest evolution of SMS. Instead of a simple text message, you can send someone an audio or video clip.

Sending a text or multimedia message

Whether you want to send a short text (SMS) message or a richer audio/video (MMS) message, the steps are similar and simple. It's message sending time! Here's how it's done:

1. **From the Home screen, press the Menu key and select Address Book.**

   Address Book opens. Alternatively, if the Address Book icon is displayed on the Home screen, simply select it.

2. **Highlight a contact with a cellphone number, press the Menu key, and select SMS or MMS *<contact name>*.**

   The menu item for SMS or MMS is intelligent enough to display the name of the contact. For example, if you choose John Doe, the menu item reads SMS John Doe or MMS John Doe. If you choose SMS, skip Step 3 and proceed directly to Step 4.

3. **Browse from your multimedia folders and select the audio or video file you want to send.**

   When choosing MMS, this extra step allows you to choose the multimedia file. This is the only difference between SMS and MMS with regards to sending a message.

4. **Type your message.**

5. **Press the Menu key and select Send.**

   Your SMS/MMS message is sent on its merry way.

Viewing or listening to a message you receive

If you have an incoming SMS or MMS message, you get notification just like you do when you receive an e-mail. Also, like e-mail, the E-mail icon on the top of the Home screen indicates the arrival of a new message. In fact, everything about viewing SMS/MMS messages is pretty much the same as what you do when reading e-mail messages; so if you have Chapter 7 loaded into *your* memory, you know how to read SMS/MMS messages.

You can customize how your BlackBerry notifies you when you receive an SMS message. Chapter 3 has the scoop on all the customization options for your BlackBerry, including options for SMS notification. (Look for the section about customizing your Profile.)

Always Online Using Instant Messaging

Real-time conversation with your friends or buddies over the Internet is easier with the advent of Instant Messenger. This technology allows two or more people to send and receive messages quickly with the use of software that uses the Internet as the wire. It all started with pure text messages and evolved into a rich medium involving voice and even video conversation in real-time.

Chatting using IM rules

When America Online (AOL) came out with Instant Messenger (IM) in the mid-1990s, it was an overnight hit. What made it successful was that it could provide quick (instantaneous) responses to any messages you sent. In addition, the service introduced many simple (yet clever) functions that offer a unique way of communicating. For example, you can chat with multiple people at the same time. You can tell whether someone is trying to type a message to you. You can even tell whether your buddies are online, away from their computers, or simply too busy to be interrupted at the moment. IM adds up to a totally different slant on long-distance communication, opening a wide array of possibilities — possibilities that can be used for good (team collaboration) or ill (mindless gossip), depending on the situation.

As you might expect, IM is great for both personal and business applications. In the business world, IM provides the link so that employees can be always connected with their colleagues, no matter how distant they might be, making working collaboratively far easier. On the personal side, this new way of keeping in touch has been embraced by a pretty broad swath of the population — not just the teen set. Whether you're busy maintaining friendships or working to create new ones, Instant Messenger is one powerful tool to consider adding to your social skills toolbox.

If your employer provides your BlackBerry Pearl, IM might not work on your device. Companies have the option of telling their network administrators to block all IM network addresses, effectively shutting you out of the IM system. If that's the case, your chances of being able to use IM on your BlackBerry Pearl are zero. (You can always get your own personal BlackBerry Pearl, though.)

IM basics: What you need

Your Blackberry Pearl comes with an IM application supporting the four leading IM networks. All you need to start using IM is a user ID and a password. If you don't have a user ID/password combo yet, getting one is a breeze. Just go to the appropriate registration Web page (listed next) for the IM network you want to use. Use your desktop or laptop machine for signing up. It's easier and faster that way.

> ✔ **AOL Instant Messenger (AIM)**
>
> http://aim.aol.com/aimnew/Aim/register.adp?
> promo=106723&pageset=Aim&client=no
>
> ✔ **ICQ Instant Messenger**
>
> http://www.icq.com/register
>
> ✔ **MSN Messenger**
>
> http://messenger.msn.com/download/getstarted.aspx
>
> ✔ **Yahoo! Instant Messenger (Y! IM)**
>
> http://edit.yahoo.com/config/eval_register?
>
> .src=pg&.done=http://messenger.yahoo.com

 Given the many IM network choices available, all your friends probably won't be registered on the same network. You might end up having to sign up for multiple networks if you want to reach them all through IM.

 If you're an avid user of GoogleTalk, don't be dismayed by not seeing it in the preceding list. RIM has a separate program that you can use. Just point Browser to this link:

```
http://www.blackberry.com/GoogleTalk/index.do
```

The page that appears gives you step-by-step instructions on how to download and install the program on your BlackBerry Pearl.

Going online with IM

After you obtain a user ID/password combo on one of the IM services, you can start chatting with your buddies by following these steps:

1. **From the Home screen, press the Menu key and select Instant Messaging.**

   A screen displaying the four popular IM services appears, as shown in Figure 8-1. You can choose from any of the four IM application icons, based on where your ID is valid.

Figure 8-1: Links to the four IM services.

2. **Highlight the IM application icon of your choice and press Enter.**

   An application-specific login screen appears for you to sign in. They're all straightforward, with the standard screen name or ID line and password line. Each screen also offers a Save Password check box; when enabled, it allows you to keep the ID/password information pre-entered next time you come back to this screen. (Um, you don't have to type this stuff every time you want to IM.) We recommend that you mark this check box to save time, but also set your handheld password enabled so that security is not compromised. Refer to Chapter 3 if you need a refresher on how to enable password on your BlackBerry.

3. **Enter your screen name or ID and password and select the Save Password check box (if desired).**

4. **Press the trackball and select Sign On.**

   At this point, IM tries to log you in. This can take a couple of seconds. After you're logged in, a simple listing of your contacts/buddies (AIM refers to contacts as *buddies*) shows up onscreen.

5. **In the list, highlight the contact/buddy you'd like to chat with, press the Menu key, and select the action you'd like from the menu that appears.**

   Your menu options are sending a message, add a contact, deleting a contact, and more.

Adding a contact/buddy

Before you can start chatting with your buddies, you need to know their user IDs as well. For AIM, you get the ID from your friend, or you can search AOL's directory. For Yahoo! users, the ID can be found on their Yahoo! e-mail addresses. (It's the text before the @ sign.) ICQ uses an ICQ number as a user ID. Again, you can always have your friend e-mail it to you or you can search the ICQ Global Directory. For MSN, you need their MSN passport ID or their Hotmail ID.

Luckily for you, you don't need to search around for IDs every time you want to IM someone. IM lets you store IDs as part of a contact list so you can grab an ID whenever you need one. To add the ID of a contact to your contact list, just do the following:

1. **Starting within the IM service of your choice, press the Menu key and select Add Buddy.**

   The Add Buddy/Contact screen appears.

2. **Enter the user ID of your buddy and then press Enter.**

   IM is smart enough to figure out whether this contact is a valid user ID or not. If the ID is valid, the application adds the ID to your list of contacts. The buddy goes to either the Online or Offline section of your list, depending on whether your buddy is logged in.

Doing the chat thing

Suppose you want to start a conversation with one of your contacts (a safe assumption on our part, we think). Just log in to the IM application, as described previously, and send a message to your buddy. By sending a message within the IM application, you're initiating a conversation. Here are all the details on how to do it:

1. **In the contacts list of the IM application of your choice, highlight the contact to whom you want to send a message, press the Menu key, and then select Send a Message.**

   A typical online chat screen shows up. The top portion of the screen lists the sequence of previous messages you sent to and received from this contact. The bottom portion of the screen is where you type your message.

2. **Enter your message.**

3. **Press the Menu key and select Send.**

   Your user ID plus the message you just sent shows up in the topmost (history) section of the chat screen. When you receive a message, it gets appended to the history section as well so that both sides of your e-conversation stay in view.

Using BlackBerry Messenger

RIM itself has entered the IM application horse race in the form of a spirited filly named — you guessed it — BlackBerry Messenger. This application is based on the PIN-to-PIN messaging technology described earlier in this chapter, which means that it is mucho fast and quite reliable. However, with BlackBerry Messenger, you can chat with only those buddies who have a BlackBerry and also have PIN-to-PIN messaging enabled. The application supports IM features common to many of the other applications, like group chatting and the capability to monitor the availability of other IM buddies.

Running BlackBerry Messenger

You can access the BlackBerry Messenger by pressing the Menu key from the Home screen and selecting BlackBerry Messenger. The very first time you run BlackBerry Messenger, the application throws up a dialog box asking you for your display name. The application also asks you to define a password in case you need to restore your contact list at some point.

The next time you open the application, you see an IM-style contact list, as shown on the left in Figure 8-2. (Okay, we know it looks pretty empty right now, but we show you how to populate it in a minute.) To customize the groupings, add a contact, set your availability, start a conversation, or change your options, just press the Menu key to call up the BlackBerry Messenger menu, as shown on the right in Figure 8-2.

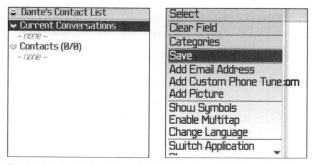

Figure 8-2: The BlackBerry Messenger contact list (left) and menu (right).

Adding a contact

With nobody in your contact list, BlackBerry Messenger is a pretty useless item. Your first order of business is to add a contact to your list — someone you know who has a BlackBerry, is entered in your Address Book, has PIN-to-PIN messaging enabled, and has a copy of BlackBerry Messenger installed on his or her device. If you know someone who fits these criteria, you can add that person to your list by doing the following:

1. **In BlackBerry Messenger, press the Menu key and select Add a Contact.**

   A listing of all the contacts in your BlackBerry Address Book shows up onscreen.

2. **Highlight the name you want to add to your BlackBerry Messenger contact list and then press the trackball.**

   The Add a Message dialog box similar to the one shown in Figure 8-3 (left) appears.

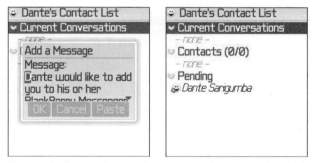

Figure 8-3: Requesting permission to add contact to BlackBerry Messenger (left). To-be-approved contacts are in the Pending group (right).

3. **Select OK from the popup.**

   Another message dialog box appears, specifying that a message was sent to your potential contact.

   Most IM applications ask a potential contact for permission to add him or her to someone's contact list. BlackBerry Messenger is no different here.

   The application sends your request for the contact to be added to your BlackBerry Messenger contact list. As long as the person has not responded to your request, his or her name appears as part of the Pending group, as shown in Figure 8-3 (right). When your contact responds positively to your request, that name is moved from the Pending group to the official contact list.

Starting a conversation

You can easily start a conversation with any of your contacts through the BlackBerry Messenger main menu:

1. **Highlight a name from your contact list, press the Menu key, and select Start Conversation.**

   A traditional chat interface appears, with a historical listing of messages at the top and a text box for typing messages at the bottom.

2. **Type your message.**

3. **Press the Enter key to send the message.**

   Any messages you send (as well as any responses you get in return) are appended to the History list at the top.

Starting a group conversation

Whenever you're conversing with someone using your BlackBerry Messenger, you can easily invite others in, as follows:

1. **Press the Menu key and select Invite.**

   This option allows you to select any number of people from your contact list one at a time from the Select a Contact screen that follows.

2. **Select the contact or contacts and then select OK.**

   You return to the previous conversation screen, but now the History list, which is the listing of your previous conversations, appends text saying that the names of your contacts have been added to the conversation. The newly selected contacts can now join in the conversation.

Chapter 9

Surfing the Internet Wave

*I*t's hard to believe that just over ten years ago, more folks didn't have access to the Internet than did. Today, you can surf the Web anytime, anywhere, and you can do it using a traditional desktop or laptop computer, or even a tiny mobile device such as a PDA or a smartphone. Having said that, it should be no surprise that your BlackBerry Pearl has a Web browser of its own.

In this chapter, we explore ways to use the BlackBerry Browser effectively. We offer shortcuts that improve your experience browsing the Web. We also throw in timesaving tips, including the coolest ways to customize your browser to make pages load faster and a complete neat-freak's guide to managing your bookmarks.

Getting Started with the BlackBerry Browser

Browser is preloaded on your BlackBerry Pearl and accesses the Web by cellphone connection. The following sections get you started using Browser. After you get your feet wet, we promise that you'll be chomping at the bit to find out more!

Accessing Browser

 You can open Browser by pressing the Menu key from the Home screen and selecting Browser. Alternatively, if you see the Browser icon from the Home screen, you can select it.

Small screen, small images

Like other similar devices, the BlackBerry has limited screen real estate and should not be compared with personal computers in terms of a Web-browsing experience. The screen is just too small to accommodate a normal Web page. Also, remember that your connection is via a cellphone network, so your connection speed varies from location to location and isn't as speedy as a Wi-Fi or cable connection. Pictures and images won't look the same, and pages might take longer to load. (The good news is that you don't have to endure nasty pop-ups.) Despite the limited capacity (compared with a traditional Web browser), when you really need information and you're away from a computer, your BlackBerry is there for you.

You can also access the Browser from any application that distinguishes a Web address. For example, from Address Book, you can scroll to a Web page field, press the trackball, and select Get Link. The Browser launches and the Web page starts opening. Also, if you get an e-mail containing a Web address, just scroll to that link. The link becomes highlighted, and you can open the page by pressing the trackball and selecting Get Link.

When you access Browser from another application (see Figure 9-1, left), you don't have to close that application to jump to Browser. Just press the Menu key, select Switch Application to bring up a pop-up screen containing application icons, and select Browser. (It's the globe icon.)

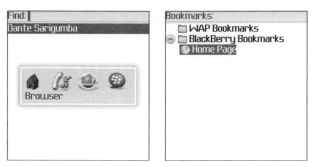

Figure 9-1: Open Browser from another application (left). The opening Browser screen (right).

By default, accessing Browser by clicking a Web address within another application opens the Web page associated with that address. Opening Browser from the Home screen menu gives you a list of bookmarks.

If you haven't yet added bookmarks, the opening Browser screen looks like the right screen in Figure 9-1. You find out more about adding bookmarks later in this chapter.

Hitting the (air)waves

After you open Browser, you're ready to surf the Web. Here's how:

1. **Open Browser.**

2. **Press the Menu key and select Go To.**

3. **In the screen that appears, enter a Web address, as shown in Figure 9-2, and then select OK.**

    The Web page appears.

Figure 9-2: Opening a Web page is simple.

When you see a phone number or an e-mail address on a Web page, you can scroll to that information to highlight it. When the information is highlighted, pressing the trackball initiates a phone call or opens a new e-mail message (depending on which type of link you highlighted).

Navigating Web pages

Using Browser to navigate a Web page is easy. Note that hyperlinks are highlighted onscreen. To jump to a particular hyperlink, scroll to the highlighted link and press the trackball.

Here are few shortcuts you can use while navigating a Web page:

- ✔ Quickly move up and down one full display page at a time by pressing 9 (down arrow) or 3 (up arrow).

- ✔ Move to the top of the page: ER key.

✔ Move to the bottom of the page: CV key.

✔ Move to the next page: M or SPACE key.

✔ Move to the previous page: UI key.

✔ Quickly switch between full-screen mode and normal mode by pressing the exclamation point (!) key. Think of full-screen mode simply as another way to view the same Web page on your BlackBerry, but the BlackBerry doesn't show anything extra (for example, signals level) on the top portion of the display screen. Normal mode is what you get by default.

✔ To stop loading a page, press the Escape key.

✔ After a page fully loads, you can go back to the previous page by pressing the Escape key.

And don't forget the Browser menu (press the Menu key). It has some useful shortcuts, as shown in Figure 9-3.

Figure 9-3: The Browser menu has lots of good stuff.

Here are the Browser menu options:

✔ **Find:** Use this option to find text within the current page. Like any other basic Find tool, choosing this option displays a prompt to enter the text you want to find. Then a Find Next menu appears after the initial search for you to use to find the next matching text.

✔ **Copy:** This menu item appears if a link is currently highlighted. Choosing this option copies text you highlighted into memory so that you can use it later for pasting elsewhere, such as your MemoPad.

✔ **Get Link:** This menu item shows up if you have a currently highlighted link. Choosing this menu item opens that page of the link. *Hint:* The faster way to open a link is to press the trackball, as mentioned earlier.

✔ **Home:** This is the shortcut to go to your home page. The default home page can vary from carrier to carrier, but you can change it by displaying the Browser menu and selecting Options, and then selecting Browser Configuration. From there, you can change the Home Page Address field.

✔ **Go To:** Choosing this allows you to open a Web page by entering the Web address and selecting OK. As you enter more addresses, the ones you entered before are listed and stored for possible future usage, to save you having to type them again. To find out how to clear that list, see the "Cache Operations" section.

✔ **Back <Esc>:** Choose this to go back to the previous page you viewed.

✔ **Forward:** If you've gone back at least one Web page in your browsing travels, use Forward to progress one page at a time.

✔ **Recent Pages:** Choosing this displays a list of the pages you have viewed previously. This is a convenient way of revisiting pages that you have just viewed.

✔ **History:** Browser can track up to 20 pages of Web addresses you've visited, which you can view on the History screen. From there, you can jump to any of those Web pages by highlighting the page and pressing the trackball.

✔ **Refresh:** Choosing this option updates the current page. This is helpful when you're viewing a page with data that changes frequently (such as stock quotes).

✔ **Set Encoding:** Choose this to specify the encoding used in viewing a Web page. This is useful when viewing foreign languages that use different characters. Most of us don't have to deal with this and probably don't know what type of encoding a particular language could display. If you have to do this, make sure you know the appropriate encoding.

At the upper-right corner of the Browser screen are a couple of icons. The rightmost icon shows the strength of the network signals (it's the same signal indicator for phone and e-mail). The icon to the left of that indicates whether you're at a secure Web page. In this case, it is a normal page. Whether a page is secure or not depends on the Web site you're visiting. If you're accessing banking information, you most likely see the secured icon (a closed lock). On the other hand, most informational pages need not be secure, so you see the unsecured icon (an open lock). *Hint:* The Web address of a secure page starts with `https` instead of `http`.

If you lose patience waiting for a page to load and want to browse somewhere else, press the Escape key to stop the page from loading.

Saving a Web page address

Entering a Web address to view a page can get tedious. Fortunately, you can return to a page without manually entering the same address. While you're viewing a Web page, simply use the Browser menu (shown on the left in Figure 9-4) to save that page's address.

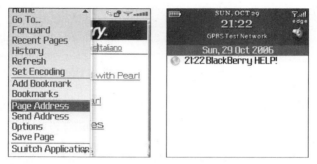

Figure 9-4: Use the Browser menu to save a Web page address (left). Save a Web page link in Messages (right).

You can save a Web page address in a couple of ways:

- ✓ **Page Address:** This option allows you to view the Web address of the current page through a pop-up screen. From this pop-up screen, you can save the page's address on your BlackBerry Clipboard and paste it in as a memo for yourself or send it to yourself or somebody else via Messages (e-mail). Convenient, right?

  When you select Send Address from the pop-up menu, you're taken to Address Book to select your e-mail recipient, and the rest is the same as sending a regular e-mail. See Chapter 7 for more on sending e-mail messages.

- ✓ **Save Page:** Use this option to save the Web address of the current page to Messages. A message appears with the Browser globe icon to indicate that it's a Web link, as shown on the right in Figure 9-4. Scrolling to that entry and pressing Enter launches Browser and opens the page for your viewing pleasure. Saving a page to your message list has a different purpose than bookmarking a page. When you save a page to your message list, you can mark the page as unread, like an e-mail message, to remind yourself to check back later.

Note: When you do not have network coverage and you try to access a Web page, you're prompted to save your request. When you do, your request is automatically saved in the message list. Then, when you do have coverage later, you can open the same Web page from the message list, and it has the loaded content already!

Pressing a letter key while you're in a menu selects the first menu item that starts with that letter. Pressing the same letter again selects the next menu item that starts with that letter.

Sending an address by e-mail

You can send a Web address to any recipient via e-mail using the Page Address option in the Browser menu. For a more *direct* way, simply select Send Address from the Browser menu while the Web page is displayed. If you know right away that you're going to send an address to someone, use the more direct method. It saves you a couple of clicks.

Saving Web images

You can view and save pictures or images from a Web page. Any saved image can be accessed using the Picture application, which enables you to view it later, even when you're out of range. To save the image from the Web page, select the image and then select Save Image from the menu that appears.

Bookmarking Your Favorite Sites

You don't have to memorize each address of your favorite sites. BlackBerry Browser allows you to keep a list of sites you want to revisit. In other words, make a *bookmark* so you can come back to a site quickly.

Adding a bookmark

On the page you want to bookmark, select Add Bookmark from the Browser menu. Remember that the menu is always accessible by pressing the Menu key. Enter the name of the bookmark and then select the folder where you want to save the bookmark in the Bookmark dialog box (as shown in Figure 9-5). The default folder is BlackBerry Bookmarks, but you can save the bookmark in folders you create. To see how to create a bookmark folder, skip to the section, "Adding a bookmark subfolder."

The next time you want to go to a bookmarked page, return to the Bookmarks screen by selecting Bookmarks from the Browser menu. From this screen, you can find all the pages you bookmarked. Just highlight the name of the bookmark and press the trackball to open that page.

Figure 9-5: Specify the name and the folder in which to store the bookmark.

Available offline

The Bookmark dialog box includes an Available Offline check box, which you might be wondering about. If that check box is checked, you not only save a page as a bookmark, you also cache it so you can view it even when you are out of network coverage (like being stuck deep in a mountain cave). The next time you click the bookmark, that page comes up very fast because Browser is retrieving the page from its cache.

If you want the latest version of the page, you have to refresh it. To do so, press the Menu key and select Refresh.

We recommend you make bookmarks to search engines (such as Google) available offline because the content of the initial search page is not likely to change from day to day.

Modifying a bookmark

Changing a bookmark is a snap:

1. **Go to the Bookmarks screen.**

   To do so, select Bookmarks from the Browser menu.

2. **Highlight the name of the bookmark you want to modify and then select Edit Bookmark from the menu.**

3. **On the screen that follows, you can edit the existing name or the address the bookmark is pointing to or both.**

4. **Click OK to save your changes.**

Organizing your bookmarks

Over time, the number of your bookmarks will grow, and having a tiny display screen can make it tough to find a certain site. To mitigate this problem, organize your bookmarks by using folders. For example, you can group related sites in a folder, and each folder can have one or more folders inside it (subfolders). In a way, you can build a tree hierarchy for your bookmarks. Having a folder hierarchy narrows down your search and allows you to easily find the site you're looking for.

Adding a bookmark subfolder

Unfortunately, you can add subfolders only to existing folders that are already listed on the Bookmarks page. Nevertheless, you can still get organized by using subfolders.

Suppose that you want to add a subfolder called *Hockey Links* within your BlackBerry Bookmarks folder. Here are the quick and easy steps to do so:

1. **On the Bookmarks screen, highlight BlackBerry Bookmarks.**

   The initial folder you highlight will be the parent of the new subfolder.

2. **Press the Menu key and select Add Subfolder.**

   You see a dialog box where you can enter the name of the folder.

3. **Enter *Hockey Links* as the name of the folder and select OK.**

   The *Hockey Links* folder appears on the Bookmarks screen bearing a folder icon.

Renaming a bookmark folder

Renaming a bookmark folder is as easy as editing a bookmark. On the Bookmarks screen, highlight the name of the folder, press the menu key, and select Rename Folder. On the screen that follows, you can edit the name of the folder. To save your changes, select OK.

Moving your bookmarks

If you keep going astray looking for a bookmark that you think exists in a particular folder but is instead in another, move that bookmark where it belongs:

1. **Highlight the bookmark, press the Menu key, and select Move Bookmark.**

2. **Use the trackball to move the bookmark to the location on the list where you want it to appear.**

3. **After you find the right location, press the trackball.**

   Your bookmark is in its new home.

Cleaning up your bookmarks

Cleaning up your bookmarks list can help you keep organized and is easy. On the Bookmarks screen, highlight the name of the bookmark you want to delete, press the Menu key, and select Delete.

You can clean up bookmarks wholesale by deleting an entire folder. However, if you delete a folder, you delete the contents of that folder as well, so purge with caution.

Browser Options and Optimization Techniques

The Browser Options screen offers three main categories of settings to choose from, as shown in Figure 9-6:

- ✔ Browser configuration
- ✔ General properties
- ✔ Cache operations

Figure 9-6: The Browser Options screen.

Browser Configuration screen

You can define browser-specific settings from the Browser Configuration screen, which you access from the Browser Options screen. The list of customization items you can amend (shown to the left of Figure 9-7) are as follows:

- **Setting up your home page.**

- **Setting the content mode you want viewed: WML, HTML, or both.** Think of *WML pages* as Web pages made just for mobile devices such as the BlackBerry. We recommend you leave this as WML or both.

- **Controlling the display of images depending on the content mode.**

- **Turning on/off the display of image placeholders if you opt to not display images.**

- **Specifying which browser type your browser emulates.** The default is BlackBerry, but Browser can emulate Microsoft Internet Explorer, Openwave (WAP), Openwave Gateway, Microsoft Pocket IE, or Netscape. We don't see much difference in behavior, so we recommend that you stick with the default BlackBerry mode.

- **Support of HTML tables.** A page with HTML tables might look different if this is disabled.

- **Use of foreground and background colors.**

- **Use of background images.**

- **Support of embedded media such as Flash and SVG.** SVG stands for *scalable vector graphics.* Think of it as Flash for mobile devices such as the BlackBerry. It can be a still image or an animated one.

- **Support of JavaScript.** A Web page might not behave normally when this option is off.

- **Enable/suppressed JavaScript pop-ups.**

- **Support of Cascading Style Sheets.**

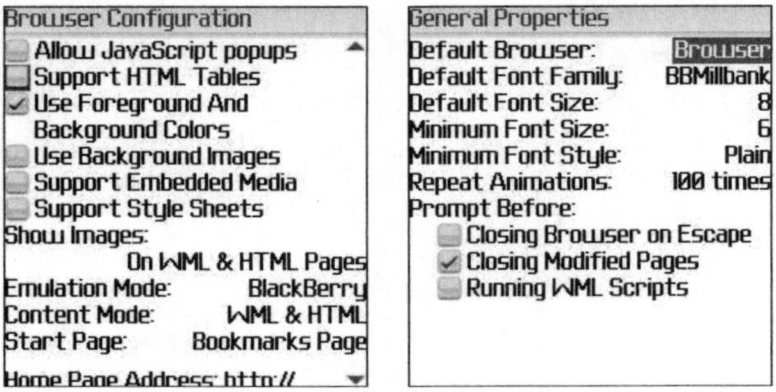

```
Browser Configuration          General Properties
  Allow JavaScript popups    ▲  Default Browser:        Browser
  Support HTML Tables           Default Font Family:    BBMillbank
✓ Use Foreground And            Default Font Size:            8
  Background Colors             Minimum Font Size:           6
  Use Background Images         Minimum Font Style:      Plain
  Support Embedded Media        Repeat Animations:   100 times
  Support Style Sheets          Prompt Before:
Show Images:                       Closing Browser on Escape
           On WML & HTML Pages  ✓ Closing Modified Pages
Emulation Mode:     BlackBerry     Running WML Scripts
Content Mode:     WML & HTML
Start Page:      Bookmarks Page
Home Page Address: http://     ▼
```

Figure 9-7: The Browser Configuration screen (left). The General Properties screen (right).

General Properties screen

The General Properties screen has the same function as the Browser Configuration screen (see the preceding section) in that you can customize some behaviors of Browser. This screen, however, is geared more toward the features of the browser content. As shown to the right of Figure 9-7, you can configure and turn on and off more features.

From this screen, you use the SPACE key to change the value of a field. You can configure the following features by selecting from the provided choices. Following this list are the General Properties screen options that you configure through on-and-off toggles.

✔ **Enable/disable prompting when closing the browser.** You can be notified before you do the following actions as a precaution:

- *Closing Browser on Escape:* Notified right before you exit BlackBerry Browser.

- *Closing Modified Pages:* Notified right before you exit a modified Web page (for example, some type of online form you fill out).

- *Running WML Scripts:* Notified right before a WML script runs.

✔ **Change the default font and font size.** You can change these settings by first highlighting them one at a time and then pressing the trackball, which displays a list of choices. Then scroll to the choice you like and press the trackball.

✔ **Set the number of times an animation repeats.** The default is 100 Times but you can change this setting to Never, Once, 10 Times, 100 Times, or as many as the image specifies.

TIP

Speeding up browsing

At times you may find that browsing the Web is extremely slow. You can make your pages load faster in exchange for not using a few features. Here are some of the techniques you can use:

- ✔ **Don't display images.** You can see a big performance improvement by turning off the display of images. From the Browser menu, select Browser Options, and then select Browser Configuration. Scroll to Show Images, and change the value to No.

- ✔ **Make sure the Pearl is not low on memory or out of memory.** When your BlackBerry is very low in memory, its performance degrades. The BlackBerry low-memory manager calls each application every now and then, telling each one to free up resources.

  Hint #1: Don't leave many e-mail messages unread. When the low-memory manager kicks in, Messages tries to delete old messages, but it can't delete those that are unread.

  Hint #2: You can also clean up the BlackBerry event log to free up needed space. Enter the letters **LGLG** while holding the Shift key. This displays an event log, where you can clear events to free up memory.

- ✔ **Turn off other features.** If you're mostly interested in viewing content, consider turning off features that pertain to how the content is processed, such as Support HTML Tables, Use Background Images, Support JavaScript, Allow JavaScript Popups, and Support Style Sheets. To turn off other browser features, go to Browser Options and select General Properties.

  Warning: We don't advise that you turn off features while performing an important task such as online banking. If you do, you might not be able to perform some of the actions on the page. For example, the Submit button might not work.

Cache operations screen

At any given time, your Blackberry uses a few cache mechanisms. When you visit a site that uses *cookies* (think of a cookie as a piece of text that a Web site created and placed in your BlackBerry's memory to remember something about you), Browser caches that cookie. Browser also caches pages and content so that you can view them offline — which is handy when you're out of range. Also, the addresses of the pages that you visited (or your latest 20 in your History list) comprise a cache. Depending on the usage of your browser, you might or might not see the Clear button(s) shown in Figure 9-8.

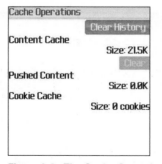

Figure 9-8: The Cache Operations options.

The size for each type of cache is displayed on this screen. If the cache has content, you will also see the Clear button, which you can use to clear the specified cache type. There are four types of cache:

- **Content Cache:** Any offline content you might have. You might want to clear this out whenever you're running out of space on your BlackBerry and need to free some memory. Or maybe when you're tired of viewing old content or tired of pressing the Refresh option.

- **Push Content:** Any content that was pushed to your Blackberry from Push Services subscriptions. You might want to clear this out to free some memory on your Blackberry.

- **Cookie Cache:** Any cookies stored on your BlackBerry. You might want to clear this out for security's sake. Sometimes you don't want a Web site to remember you.

- **History:** This is the list of sites you've visited using the Go To function. You might want to clear this for the sake of security if you don't want other people knowing which Web sites you're visiting on your BlackBerry.

Chapter 10

Calling Your Favorite Person

. . . .

In This Chapter

▶ Accessing the BlackBerry Phone application

▶ Making calls and receiving them

▶ Managing your calls with call forwarding, and more

▶ Customizing your BlackBerry Phone setup

▶ Conferencing

▶ Talking hands-free on your BlackBerry phone

▶ Multitasking with your BlackBerry phone

. . . .

*P*hone capability has been incorporated into BlackBerry from the very first generations of the device. The great news is that the BlackBerry phone operates no differently than any other phone you've used.

So why bother with this chapter? Although your BlackBerry phone operates like any other phone you've used, it has capabilities that far outreach those of your run-of-the-mill cellphone. For example, when was the last time your phone was connected to your to-do list? Have you ever received an e-mail and placed a call directly from that e-mail? We didn't think so. But with your BlackBerry Pearl, you can do all these things and more.

In this chapter, we first cover phone basics and then show you some of the neat ways BlackBerry Phone intertwines with other BlackBerry applications and functions.

Using the BlackBerry Phone Application

Accessing the Phone application from the Pearl is a snap. From the Home screen, pressing any of the numeric keys brings you right into the BlackBerry Phone application. Or, if you prefer, you can press the green Send button located right below the display screen to get into the Phone application.

Making and Receiving Calls

The folks at RIM have created an intuitive user interface to all the essential Phone features, including making and receiving calls.

Making a call

To make a call, start from the Home screen and type the number you want to dial. As soon as you start typing numbers, the Phone application opens. When you've finished typing the destination number, press the green Send key.

Calling from the Address Book

Because you can't possibly remember all your friends' and colleagues' phone numbers, calling from the Address Book is convenient and useful.

To call from the Address Book, follow these steps:

1. **Open the Phone application.**

2. **Press the Menu key.**

   The Phone menu appears, as shown in Figure 10-1.

Call From Address Book	
Call Voice Mail	
Call Work	
Call Home	
Email Dante Sarigumba	55
SMS Dante Sarigumba	
View History	) 20:53
Remove Speed Dial	18:01
Delete	10/23
View Speed Dial List	10/23
View Contact	
Options	
Status	

Figure 10-1: The Phone menu.

3. **Select Call from Address Book.**

   Address Book opens. From here, you can search as usual for the contact you'd like to call.

4. **From Address Book, highlight your call recipient and press the trackball to select Call.**

   This makes the call.

Dialing letters

One of the nice features of the BlackBerry Phone is that you can dial letters, and BlackBerry will figure out the corresponding number. For example, to dial 1-800-11-LEARN, do the following on your BlackBerry:

1. **From the Phone application (or the Home screen), dial 1-8-0-0-1-1.**

   As you type the first number, the Phone application opens (if it isn't open already) and displays the numbers you dialed.

2. **Press and hold the Alt key and then dial (press) L-E-A-R-N.**

   The letters appear onscreen as you type.

3. **Press the green Send key.**

   This call is initiated.

Receiving a call

Receiving a call on your Pearl is even easier than making a call. You can receive calls in a couple of ways. One is by using your Pearl's automated answering feature, and the other is by answering the calls manually.

Automated answering is triggered whenever you take your BlackBerry out from your holster; in other words, just taking the BlackBerry out forces it to automatically pick up any call, so you can start talking right away. The disadvantage of this is that you don't have time to see who is calling you (on your caller ID).

Note: To disable auto-answering, just be sure your BlackBerry isn't in its holster when an incoming call arrives.

What's the advantage of disabling auto-answering? Well, manual answering prompts you to answer a call or ignore a call when you receive an incoming call, as shown in Figure 10-2. This way, you can see on your caller ID who is calling you, before you decide to pick up or ignore the call.

Figure 10-2: Ignore or answer with manual answering.

Phone Options While on a Call

When you're on the phone, situations might arise where you'd want to mute your conversation or change the call volume. No problem. BlackBerry Pearl makes such adjustments easy.

Muting your call

You might want to use the mute feature while on a conference call (see the upcoming section, "Arranging Conference Calls") when you don't need to speak but do need to hear what is being discussed. Maybe you're on the bus or have kids in the background, making your surroundings noisy. But by using mute, all the background noises are filtered out from the conference call.

To mute your call. follow these steps:

1. **While in a conversation, press the Menu key.**

   The Phone menu appears in all its glory.

2. **Select Mute.**

   You will hear a tone sound, indicating that your call is on mute.

To un-mute your call:

1. **While a call is on mute, press the Menu key.**

   The Phone menu makes another appearance.

2. **Select Turn Mute Off.**

   You will hear a tone sound, indicating that your call is now un-muted.

Adjusting the call volume

Adjusting the call volume, a simple yet important action on your BlackBerry phone, can be performed by simply pressing the volume up or down key on the side of your Pearl.

Customizing the BlackBerry Phone

For your BlackBerry Phone to work the way you like, you have to first set it up the way you want it. In this section, we go through some settings that can make you the master of your BlackBerry Phone.

Setting up your voice mail number

This section shows you how to set up your voice mail access number. Unfortunately, the instructions for setting up your voice mailbox vary, depending on your service provider. Fortunately, however, most service providers are more than happy to walk you through the steps to get your mailbox set up in a jiffy.

To set up your voice mail number:

1. **Open the Phone application, press the Menu key, and select Options.**

   A list of phone options appears.

2. **Select Voice Mail.**

   This opens the voice mail configuration screen.

3. **Scroll to access the number field and enter your voice mail access number.**

4. **Confirm your changes by pressing the Menu key and selecting Save.**

   If this field is empty and you don't know this number, contact your service provider and ask for your voice mail access number.

Using call forwarding

On the BlackBerry, you have two types of call forwarding:

- **Forward All Calls:** Any calls to your BlackBerry are forwarded to the number you designate. Another name for this feature is *unconditional forwarding*.

✔ **Forward Unanswered Calls:** Calls that meet different types of conditions are forwarded to different numbers.

For the unanswered calls type of forwarding, three conditions determine what number to forward to:

✔ **If Busy:** You don't have call waiting turned on, and you're on the phone.

✔ **If No Answer:** You don't hear your phone ring or somehow are unable to pick up your phone (perhaps you're in a meeting).

✔ **If Unreachable:** You're out of network coverage and cannot receive any signals.

Out of the box, your BlackBerry Pearl forwards any unanswered calls, regardless of conditions, to your voice mail number by default. However, you can add new numbers to forward a call to.

You need to be within network coverage before can you change your call forwarding option. After you're within network coverage, you can change your call forwarding settings by doing the following:

1. **Open the Phone application, press the Menu key, and select Options.**

   A list of phone options appears.

2. **Select Call Forwarding.**

   Your BlackBerry now attempts to connect with the server. If successful, you'll see the Call Forwarding screen.

   If you don't see the Call Forwarding screen, wait until you have network coverage and try again.

3. **From the Call Forwarding screen, press the Menu key and select Edit Numbers.**

   A list of number(s) appears. If this is the first time you're setting call forwarding, most likely only your voice mail number is on this list.

4. **To add a new forwarding number, press the Menu key and select New Number.**

   A pop-up menu appears, prompting you to enter the new forwarding number.

5. **In the pop-up window, enter the number you want to forward to and then press the trackball.**

   The new number you entered now appears on the call forward number list. You can add this new number to any call forwarding types or conditions.

6. Press the Escape key.

You are returned to the Call Forwarding screen.

7. Scroll to the If Unreachable field and press the trackball.

A drop-down menu appears listing numbers from the call forwarding number list, including the one you just added.

8. Select the number you want to forward to and then press the trackball.

Doing so places the selected number into the If Unreachable field. You can see this on the call forwarding screen.

9. Confirm your changes by pressing the Menu key and selecting Save.

Configuring speed dial

Speed dial is a convenient feature on any phone. And after you get used to having it on a phone system, it's hard not to use it on other phones, including your BlackBerry phone.

Viewing your speed dial list

To view your speed dial list:

1. Open the Phone application.

2. Press the Menu key and select View Speed Dial List.

This displays a list of speed dial entries, as shown in Figure 10-3. If you haven't set up any speed dials, this list will be empty.

Adding a new number to speed dial

Setting up speed dial numbers is as easy as using them. It takes a few seconds to set them up, but you benefit every time you use this feature.

To assign a number to a speed dial slot, follow these steps:

1. Open the Phone application.

2. Press the Menu key, select Options, and then select View Speed Dial List.

This brings up the list of speed dial numbers you have.

3. Scroll to an empty speed dial slot, press the Menu key, and select New Speed Dial.

The BlackBerry Address Book appears so you can select a contact's phone number.

```
Speed Dial Numbers
1  Voice Mail 5198884369
2  Rob Kao (H) 9089900909
3  212.333.2222
4  Rob Kao (W) 2122223322
5  Dante Sarigu... (H) 2125551111
6
7
8
9
!
?
.
,
```

Figure 10-3: The speed dial list.

4. Select a contact, and then press the trackball.

The number appears in the speed dial list.

If more than one number is associated with the selected contact in the Address Book, you're prompted to select which number to add to the speed dial list.

Using speed dial

After you have a few speed dial entries set up, you can start using them. While at the Home screen or Phone application, press a speed dial key. The call is initiated to the number associated with that particular speed dial key.

Arranging Conference Calls

To have two or more people on the phone with you — the infamous conference call — do the following:

1. Use the Phone application to place a call to the first participant.

2. While the first participant is on the phone with you, press the Menu key and select New Call.

This automatically places the first call on hold and brings up a new call screen, as shown in Figure 10-4, prompting you to place another call.

3. Place a call to the second participant by dialing a number, pressing the trackball, and then selecting Call.

You can either dial the number using the number pad, or you can select a frequently dialed number from your call log. To place a call from your Address Book, press the trackball from the New Call screen and choose Call from Address Book. Your BlackBerry then prompts you to select a contact to dial to from the Address Book.

Figure 10-4: The New Call screen, with a meeting participant on hold.

This is just like any other phone call (except that the first participant is still on the other line).

4. **While the second participant is on the phone with you, press the Menu key and select Join, as shown in Figure 10-5.**

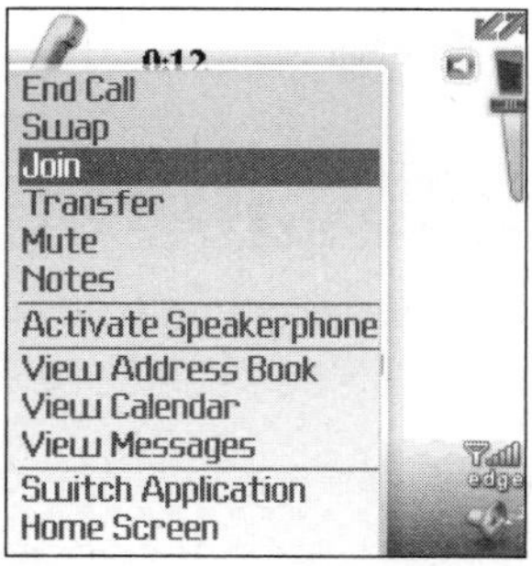

Figure 10-5: Join two people in a conference call.

This reconnects the first participant back with you, along with the second participant. Now you can discuss away with both participants at the same time.

Another name for having two people on the phone with you is *three-way calling,* which is not a new concept. If you want to chat with four people or even ten people on the phone at the same time, you certainly can. Simply repeat Steps 2 through 4 in the preceding list until you have all the participants on the phone conference.

Talking privately to a conference participant

During a conference call, you might want to talk to one participant privately. This is called *splitting* your conference call. Here's how you do it:

1. **While on a conference call, press the Menu key and select Split.**

   This brings up a pop-up screen, listing all the participants of the conference call. (See Figure 10-6.)

Figure 10-6: All the participants in the conference call.

2. **From the pop-up screen, select the participant with whom you want to speak privately.**

   This action places all other participants on hold and connects you to the participant that you selected. On the display screen, you can see to whom you are connected — this confirms that you selected the right person to privately chat with.

3. **To talk to all participants again, press the Menu key and select Join.**

   Doing so brings you back to the conference call with everyone.

Alternate between phone conversations

Whether you're in a private conversation during a conference call or you're talking to someone while you have someone else on hold, you can switch between the two conversations by swapping them. Follow these steps:

1. **While talking to someone with another person on hold, press the Menu key and select Swap.**

   Doing so switches you from the person with whom you're currently talking to the person who was on hold.

2. **Repeat Step 1 to go back to the original conversation.**

Dropping that meeting hugger

If you've been on conference calls, you can identify those chatty "meeting huggers" who have to say something about everything. Don't you wish that you could drop them off the call? Well, with your Pearl, you can (as long as you are the meeting moderator or the person who initiates the call).

1. **While on a conference call, press the Menu key and select Drop Call.**

   This brings up a pop-up screen, listing all the participants of the conference call.

2. **From the pop-up screen, select the meeting hugger you want to drop.**

   Doing so disconnects the meeting hugger.

3. **Conversation can continue as usual.**

Communicating Hands-Free

Because more and more places prohibit the use of mobile phones without a hands-free headset, we thought we'd go through the hands-free options you have on your BlackBerry.

Using the speaker phone

The Speaker Phone function is useful under certain situations, such as when you're in a room full of people who want to join in on your phone conversation. Or, you might be all by your lonesome in your office but are stuck rooting through your files — hard to do with a BlackBerry scrunched up against your ear. (We call such moments *multitasking* — a concept so important we devote an entire upcoming section to it.)

To switch to the Speaker Phone while you're on a phone call, press the OP key or press the Menu key and select Activate Speaker Phone.

Pairing your BlackBerry with a Bluetooth headset

Since your BlackBerry comes with a wired hands-free headset, you can start using it by simply plugging it into the headset jack on the left side of your BlackBerry. You adjust the volume of the headset using the volume keys (on the side of the Pearl).

Using the wired hands-free headset can help you avoid being a police target, but if you're multitasking on your BlackBerry, the wired headset can get in the way and become inconvenient.

This is where the whole Bluetooth wireless thing comes in. You can purchase a BlackBerry Bluetooth headset to go with your Bluetooth-enabled BlackBerry. For a list of BlackBerry-compatible Bluetooth headsets, see Chapter 16.

After you purchase a BlackBerry-compatible Bluetooth headset, you can pair it with your BlackBerry. Think of *pairing* a Bluetooth headset with your BlackBerry as registering the headset with your BlackBerry so that it recognizes the headset.

First things first: You need to prep your headset for pairing. Now, each headset manufacturer has a different take on this, so you'll need to consult your headset documentation for details. With that out of the way, though, you'll need to continue with the pairing. Here's how that's done:

1. **From the Home screen, press the Menu key and select Bluetooth.**

2. **Press the Menu key to display the Bluetooth menu.**

   You see the Enable Bluetooth option. If you see the Disable Bluetooth option instead, you can skip to Step 4.

3. **From the menu, scroll to Enable Bluetooth and press the trackball.**

   This enables Bluetooth on your BlackBerry.

4. **Press the Menu key to display the Bluetooth menu and select Add Device.**

   You see the Searching for Devices progress bar, um, progressing, as shown in Figure 10-7 (left). When your BlackBerry discovers the headset, a Select Device dialog box appears with the name of the headset, as shown in Figure 10-7 (right).

5. **From the Select Device dialog box, select the Bluetooth headset.**

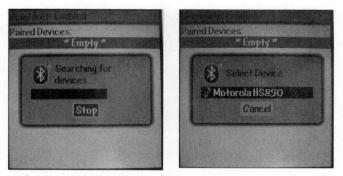

Figure 10-7: Searching for a headset (left). Success! A headset (right).

A dialog box appears to prompt you for a passkey code to the headset.

6. Enter the passkey and press the trackball.

Normally, the passkey is 0000, but refer to your headset documentation. After you successfully enter the passkey, you see your headset listed in the Bluetooth setting screen.

7. Press the Menu key to display the Bluetooth menu and select Connect.

Your BlackBerry now attempts to connect to the Bluetooth headset.

8. When you see a screen like Figure 10-8, you can start using your Bluetooth headset.

Figure 10-8: You can begin using your Bluetooth headset.

Using voice dialing

 With your headset and the Voice Dialing application, you can truly be hands-free from your Pearl. You might be thinking, "How do I activate the Voice Dialing application without touching the Pearl?" Good question. The majority of hands-free headsets (Bluetooth or not) come with a multipurpose button.

After your headset is active, press its multipurpose button to activate the Voice Dialing application. You will be greeted with a voice stating, "Say a command." At this point, simply say "Call *name of person* or *number*." The Voice Dialing application is quite good in recognizing the name of the person and the numbers you dictate. We strongly suggest that you try the voice dialing feature before you need it (for example, while driving).

Multitasking While on the Phone

One of the great things about the BlackBerry Pearl is that you can use it for other tasks while you're on the phone. For example, while on a phone call, you can take notes or make a to-do list. Or you can look up a phone number in BlackBerry Address Book that your caller is asking you for. You can even compose an e-mail while on a call.

It only makes sense to multitask while you're using a hands-free headset or a speaker phone. Otherwise, your face would be stuck to your BlackBerry, and you couldn't engage in your conversation and multitask at the same time.

After you have your hands-free headset on or a speaker phone turned on, you can start multitasking by doing the following:

1. **While in a conversation, from the Phone application, press the Menu key and select Home Screen.**

   Alternatively, you can simply press the Esc button while in the Phone application to return to your Home screen. This returns you to the Home screen without terminating your phone conversation.

2. **From the Home screen, you can start multitasking.**

Although you can compose e-mails during a phone conversation, you can't send the e-mail until you finish the phone conversation. In addition, you can't surf the Web while on the phone.

While on the phone and multitasking, however, you can still access the Phone menu from other applications. For example, from your to-do list, you can end a call or put a call on hold.

Chapter 11

Taking Great Pictures with Your Pearl

In This Chapter

▶ Zooming, using the flash, taking shots, and more

▶ Saving, viewing, and organizing your pictures

▶ Sharing your pictures

▶ Setting a picture as a caller ID or Home screen image

*P*earl is the first BlackBerry with a built-in camera, and we bet it's one of the reasons you have one, right? So, hold your breath as we go to the depths on how you can take advantage of this great feature. This will be a fun chapter. Not only that, we'll walk you through the steps in capturing that funny pose. Plus, we'll also advance your knowledge on the tricks for taking the best shots and show you how to store those shots and share them with your buddies.

Say Cheese

Before you ask someone to pose, let's examine your BlackBerry first. Your finger is not blocking the lens, check (the lens is located on the back side of your BlackBerry). The camera is active, check. It's not? You see the bottom key on the right side of your BlackBerry? That's the key to the kingdom; let's call it the camera key. Press it and you'll see the camera screen appears. Alternatively, you can open the camera by pressing the Menu key from the Home screen and selecting Camera.

C'mon, try it! After the camera is active, you should see the image in the screen that the camera is going to capture. Pressing the camera key again will capture that image. Ready? Press the camera key. You should hear a funky sound emulating the shutter of a regular camera. Neat and easy, isn't it?

Hey, you can take a picture of yourself as well. Turn that BlackBerry back and you should see a mirror right below the lens. Whatever you see in that mirror is what the camera captures.

Itching to take more pictures? Hold your horses. Take a few moments first to familiarize yourself with the camera's features.

The Screen Indicators

When you open the Camera application, the first thing you see is the screen shown in Figure 11-1. The top portion of this screen allows you to see the image you're about to capture. The bottom part contains icons (starting from the left) that indicate the number of pictures you can capture, focusing, and flash. Prepare to dissect.

Figure 11-1: The Camera screen ready to take pictures.

Choosing picture quality

Your camera is capable of capturing up to 1.3 megapixels of resolution. You probably don't need this much resolution because it also requires a bigger space to save your image. So, your BlackBerry allows you to set three picture qualities: namely Normal, Fine, and

SuperFine. The default setting is Normal, which is the lowest quality but gives you the largest number of pictures you can save — 200.

The tradeoff of using Normal is that it may not be as smooth or fine compared to the Fine and SuperFine settings. You should choose a setting based on how you plan to use the picture. If you're taking a shot of a breathtaking landscape in which you want to capture every possible detail and print it later, you'll want the SuperFine setting. On the other hand, if you're just taking pictures of your friends' faces so you can attach them as Caller ID, Normal is appropriate.

Changing picture quality is a snap. Here's how:

1. **Open the Camera application.**

   From the Home screen, press the Menu key and select Camera.

2. **Press the Menu key and select Options.**

3. **Highlight Picture Quality and press the SPACE key.**

   Pressing the SPACE key toggles the picture quality value between Normal, Fine, and SuperFine. You may have to press the SPACE key twice to select the setting you want.

4. **Press the Menu key and select Save.**

   The picture quality you've chosen is now active.

Zooming and focusing

Focus! We mean your camera. You need to be steady to get a good focus while taking the shots. Although it's convenient to use one hand while taking pictures, you would soon discover that most of the time you'll get a blurry image. Our advice is to use both hands, one holding the BlackBerry steady and the other clicking the button. This is even more important if you're zooming in. Yes, your camera is capable of up to 5x digital zoom. Use the trackball for this; scrolling up zooms in and scrolling down zooms out. While using the zoom, the value in the indicator changes from 1x, 2x, up to 5x and vice versa, depending on the direction of your scroll.

When zooming, your thumb is already on the trackball. What a convenient way to take the picture — just press.

Setting the flash

The rightmost indicator on the Camera screen is the flash. The default is Automatic, which shows an arrow with the letter *A*.

Automatic means it detects the amount of light you have at the moment you capture the image. Where it's dark, the flash fires; otherwise it will not. You can also turn it ON or OFF. When set to OFF, the arrow image is encircled with a diagonal line, just like you see on the Don't Walk traffic signal. You can toggle the settings in Camera's Options screen, which is accessible by pressing the Menu key.

Working with Pictures

You've amassed pictures and you want to view, delete, or perhaps organize them. No problem.

Viewing

Viewing a picture is one of the common functions you're going to do in your camera. And it's also one of the default behaviors. After taking a picture, right then and there, the screen changes to view mode, allowing you to see the image you just captured, as shown in Figure 11-2. If you happened to be browsing through your picture folders, you can view an individual picture by highlighting it and pressing the trackball.

Slide show

While viewing the list of pictures in a folder, press the Menu key and select Slide Show. Voila! Your BlackBerry displays your pictures one at a time at a regular time interval. The default interval between each picture is 2 seconds; if you're not happy with this interval, change it in the Options screen. Again, the Options screen is available by pressing the Menu key and selecting Options.

Trashing

If you don't like the image you captured, you can delete it. Just highlight the picture you want trashed and press the DEL key, then select Delete from the confirmation screen that follows. Note that you can do the same right after taking the picture; just click the trash can icon (refer to Figure 11-2).

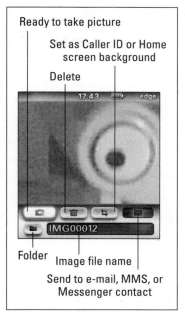

Ready to take picture

Set as Caller ID or Home
screen background

Delete

Folder

Image file name

Send to e-mail, MMS, or
Messenger contact

Figure 11-2: The Camera screen after taking a picture.

Listing

The default setting when you open a folder packed with pictures is
a listing of *thumbnails,* which are a small previews of your pictures.
Preview is nice, but if you're trying to search for a picture file and
know the file name, wouldn't it be nice if you just saw the listing of
names instead of the thumbnails? While you're in a folder, press
the trackball and select View List. That's exactly what you get: a
listing of all the pictures in this folder. What's neat is that it also
displays the size of the file.

Picture properties

Curious about the amount of memory your picture is taking? Or
maybe you just want to know the time you took it. While highlighting the picture from a list or viewing it, press the Menu key and
select Properties. What you'll see next is a screen similar to Figure
11-3. This screen displays the location of your picture, the size of
the file, and when it was last modified.

```
..e Memory/home/user/pictures/
   Up
   IMG00012.jpg          50.17k
                         02k
      /Device Memory/home/
      user/pictures/Beauty  .71k
      and the beast.jpg    32k
      Size:       37.21k   29k
      Image File           02k
      Last Modified:       36k
         23 Oct 2006 12:38 02k
   IMG00002.jpg          37.21k
   Beauty and the bea...  37.21k
```

Figure 11-3: Your picture properties.

Organizing your pictures

You might be interested in putting some order into where your pictures are stored and how they are named. Organization is all about time and the best use of it. After all, you want to enjoy looking *at* your pictures — not looking *for* them. BlackBerry enables you to rename and move pictures to different folders. Plus, you can create folders too. With those capabilities, you should be on your way to organization nirvana.

Renaming a picture

While capturing a picture, the image is actually saved in your BlackBerry. However, the name is a bit generic, something like IMG000x. You should make a habit to rename it as soon as you've finished capturing it. It is easier to recognize *Dean blows birthday candles* than *IMG0029*. Renaming is a snap. Here's how:

1. **While the picture is viewed on the screen or highlighted in the list, press the Menu key and select Rename.**

   A Rename screen appears, as shown in Figure 11-4.

2. **Enter the name you want for this picture and then select OK.**

   Your picture has been renamed.

Creating a new folder

Being the organized person you are, you must be wondering about the folders we mentioned. Don't fret, it's quite simple to create one. Here's how:

1. **In the Camera screen, press the Menu key and select View Pictures.**

The screen displays the list of pictures in the current folder and an Up icon for you to navigate up to the folder above this folder.

Figure 11-4: Rename your picture here.

2. **Select the Up icon to navigate to the main folder in which you want your new folder to be created.**

   You should be within the folder where you want your new folder to be created. If not, repeat this step and use your trackball to navigate to that folder.

3. **Press the Menu key and select New Folder.**

4. **Enter the name of the folder and select OK.**

   Your folder is created.

Moving pictures

There are many reasons for moving pictures between folders and one of them is the obvious: organization. Want to try it? Follow these steps:

1. **In the Camera screen, press the Menu key and select View Pictures.**

   The screen displays the list of pictures in the current folder. If the picture you want to move is not in this folder, click the Up icon to navigate up to other folders.

2. **Highlight the picture you want to move, press the Menu key, and select Move.**

   The screen that follows allows you to navigate to the folder where you want to move this picture.

3. **Click the Up icon and use the trackball to navigate to the folder where you want to move this picture.**

4. Press the Menu key and select Move Here.

Your picture is moved.

Sharing your pictures

There's no joy in taking great pictures if you're the only one seeing them, right? Your BlackBerry Pearl has a couple of options for sharing your bundle of joy. Highlight one of those pictures, and then press the Menu key. You should see the following options:

- ✓ **Send As Email:** This option goes directly to the compose e-mail screen, with the currently selected picture as an attachment.

- ✓ **Send to Messenger Contact:** This option displays a screen with a list of your BlackBerry Messenger contacts. This allows you to choose the contact to whom you want to send the selected picture.

- ✓ **Send As MMS:** Similar to Send As Email, this opens a compose MMS screen with the currently selected picture as an attachment. The only difference is that it will first display the Address Book, letting you select the person's phone number to receive the MMS before proceeding to the compose screen.

- ✓ **Send Using Bluetooth:** This will allow you to send the picture to any device that is capable of communicating through Bluetooth. See Chapter 10 for details on how to enable and pair Bluetooth devices.

Setting a picture as the caller ID

Wouldn't it be nice if when you received a call from someone, his or her picture appeared on the screen? Yup, you can do that. If you have the face of your buddy inside your BlackBerry, view it (see the previous section on viewing pictures), press the Menu key, and select Set as Caller ID. (If you don't have pictures of your friends, now is the time to show off your gem and start clicking.)

Setting a Home screen image

Suppose you have a stunning picture that you want to use as the background image of your BlackBerry. Just view the picture (see the previous discussion on viewing pictures), press the Menu key, and select Set As Home Screen Image. You can always reset the home screen image by going back to the same menu screen and selecting Reset Home Screen Image.

Other Important Camera Options

The camera in your BlackBerry is a piece of hardware and a computer program. It is therefore within the bounds of your BlackBerry's available memory. As such, the good people at RIM incorporated some parameters that you can set so that you'll enjoy the use of your camera fully and, at the same time, not affect other important features that share the same memory resource. Following are two important option settings you need to know:

- **Device Memory Limit:** The amount of device memory your camera can use. The values are 12M, 15M, 20M, and 25M (1M is 1000K). To get a feel for how many pictures this is, look at the properties of an existing picture and note its file size.

- **Reserved Pictures Memory:** The amount of memory BlackBerry reserves for the camera to store pictures. Possible values are 0M, 2M, 5M, 8M, 10M, and 12M. This value can't be set greater than the Device Memory Limit.

If you open the Camera application and see "Could not start the camera. Close other applications and try opening the camera again" message, it means your BlackBerry is running out of memory for the camera to run smoothly. One solution is to follow what the message says. Press the Shift and the Escape keys at the same time and a list of applications appears. (The Escape key is to the right of the trackball and has the curving arrow symbol.) Go through these applications and close them. If this doesn't work, the all-reliable reset (taking the battery out and putting it back in) is your ultimate solution.

Chapter 12

Satisfy All Your Senses with the Media Player

In This Chapter
▶ Listening and viewing media
▶ Importing your PC media collections
▶ Downloading media

*I*f there is a word to describe today's phone market trends, it's convergence. Your BlackBerry Pearl is one of the latest participants of this convergence race. We probably don't have to tell you this, but in addition to being a phone, e-mail, camera, and PDA device, your Pearl is a portable media player. In the palm of your hand, you will be able to listen to music, watch video clips, sample ringtones, and view pictures. These are all bundled into an application with a name you would recognize even after consuming a couple of pints of strong ale – Media. This chapter is all about Media and how you can take advantage of its capabilities.

Accessing Media

To run Media, simply press the Menu key from the Home screen and select Media. Or if you have it chosen as one of the five applications you display in the Home screen, you can select it directly by clicking its icon.

Media is a collection of media types: Music, Video, Ringtones, and Pictures, as shown in Figure 12-1. You don't need to be Einstein to figure out what each one of these media types is for. Ready to have some fun?

Figure 12-1: Explore Media here.

Folder navigation

Whether you want to play music, watch a video clip, test a ring-tone, or view pictures from your BlackBerry, you have to navigate to the location of your media files. Media files are stored in three types of memory locations, namely Media Card, Device Memory, and Preloaded Media. You have the option to read and write the Media Card and the Device Memory locations. However, the Preloaded Media location can be only read and not written. All we care about is how to navigate and find your media files.

These memory locations are organized in folders, as shown in Figure 12-2. To navigate inside, simply select the folder. A folder may contain subfolders, so you can keep opening down until you find the files you want. To move up the folder hierarchy, select Up.

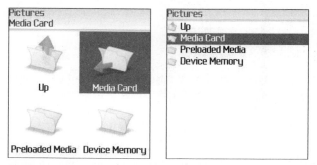

Figure 12-2: The folders to media files, with thumbnails view (left) and list view (right).

Let the music play

To play music in your BlackBerry Pearl, you don't need a quarter. Just select Music from Media screen and a folder structure similar to the one shown on the right in Figure 12-2 appears, with Music as the heading of the screen instead of Pictures. Navigate through this folder structure to find the music file you want.

After you find the file, simply select it and it will begin playing, with a screen as shown in Figure 12-3. BlackBerry Pearl supports many music formats (with file extensions) including:

- ✔ **ACC:** Audio compression formats AAC, AAC+, and EAAC+ (`.aac`, `.m4a`)

- ✔ **AMR:** Adaptive Multi Rate-Narrow Band (AMR-NB) speech coder standard (`.mmr`, `.3gp`)

- ✔ **MIDI:** Polyphonic MIDI (`.mid`, `.midi`, `.smf`)

- ✔ **WAV:** Wave files (`.wav`)

- ✔ **MP3:** MPEG Part 1 and Part 2 audio layer 3 (`.mp3`, `.mp4`)

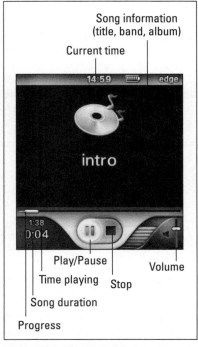

Figure 12-3: The music plays here.

Making your video files play in Pearl

When you try playing an existing video file in your BlackBerry Pearl, the likelihood that it will fail playing is high. The common reason is that most video files are encoded to play on a bigger screen. Not to worry. With the help of your PC and something called an encoder, you can easily convert these files into a format that's friendly to your Pearl. You can download many types of encoders from the Web. We found *Super,* a free encoder that does a decent job and supports many file types. Here's the link to download Super:

```
http://www.blackberryfordummies.com/pearl/super.html
```

After you've downloaded and installed Super onto your PC, you're ready to convert your video files. Launch Super. The screen that follows might be a bit intimidating, but relax. Without going into too much detail on the numbers and fields, we'll give you quick settings to use:

- ✔ Output Container: **avi**
- ✔ Output Video Codec: **H.263**
- ✔ Aspect: **11.9**
- ✔ Frame/Sec: **14.985**
- ✔ Bitrate kbps: **576**

Leave the default values for the rest of the fields. Next, you need to tell Super the location of the file you want to encode and where you want the output file. You can do this by right-clicking anywhere on the Super screen, selecting Add Multimedia File(s), and navigating to your video file. Then right-click again, select Specify the Output Folder Destination, and navigate to that folder. Then click Encode (Active Job-List Files). That's it! Super encodes the file, and makes it smaller. Now you can copy this file to your media card and enjoy watching it from your BlackBerry Pearl.

Selecting each file to play sometimes could be a hassle — and not even a sensible thing to do if you're in a gym or jogging. Fret not. You would have asked for this feature in the first place, so RIM added an option for you to play all songs within a folder or even all subfolders. While you are in a folder, press the Menu key and select Play All to play every song in the current folder and all sub-folders, or select Play Folder to play songs in the current folder.

Note that there is no fast forwarding or rewinding.

 The earpiece combo mike that comes with BlackBerry Pearl is only for one ear. This might be an issue when you are in a noisy area. To improve your experience, you can buy a stereo headset. And, yes, a Bluetooth headset is a good option.

Now showing

To play video clips, the general steps are no different than playing music files. Just select Video from Media screen and again a screen similar to Figure 12-2 appears, but with Video as the heading instead of Pictures. Navigate to the video file you want, select it, and a contender to the funniest home video is playing. Video formats supported are .avi, .mov, .mp4, and .3gp. Start collecting now.

Similar to Music, if you press the Menu key in one of the folders containing video files, you can select Play All to play every video file in the current folder and all its subfolders, or select Play Folder to play every video file in only the current folder.

Note that there is no fast forwarding or rewinding.

Lord of the ringtones

Ah, the proliferation of ringtones; that's history. Nothing beats hearing a loud funky ringtone while you're sleeping on a bus or a train. Whether you want a real Matchbox Twenty's "3 A.M." song or the old-fashioned digital repercussions or anything that would annoy the guy sitting next to you, you have that flexibility. Give a toast to BlackBerry Pearl. Of course you want to hear ringtones that come with your BlackBerry Pearl. And, there's a bunch, so enjoy.

Simply select Ringtones from the Media screen. What you see next is the same navigation screen that Music and Video use (refer to Figure 12-2). Again, your BlackBerry Pearl comes with a decent selection of ringtones, stored in Preloaded Media. You can select this folder or a folder where you've stored any ringtones you've acquired. After you are in a folder showing a list of ringtones, select one from the list and it will start playing. You can also play all the ringtones in the folder by pressing the Menu key and selecting either Play Folder or Play All, which is the same as Play Folder but includes all the ringtones in the subfolders.

If you find a ringtone you like, you can make it the default ring by highlighting it, pressing the Menu key, and selecting Set As Phone Tune. A ringtone is similar to a music file and includes the following music formats: .aac, .mmr, .m4a, .midi, .mp3.

Picture this

Folks who upgraded from an older BlackBerry may know Picture. It's one of the intuitive applications RIM kept in BlackBerry Pearl but made better. Picture, as the name implies, allows you to view images, with zoom and rotate capabilities.

Select Picture from Media screen and what you see next is the familiar folder structure. Navigate to the folder structure where your pictures are stored. After you find the picture file, just select it. Easy does it, right?

Check out Preloaded Media. Your BlackBerry Pearl comes with nice pictures you can use as the background image of the Home screen. There are also some cartoon images that you can temporarily assign to your contacts as caller IDs until you get a chance to take their pictures.

Zoom to details

Is that a pimple? No, it's not. Let's zoom in. While viewing an image, press the trackball and select Zoom. A tiny nonobtrusive slider bar appears on the left side of the image. Now, use your trackball: scrolling up will zoom in and scrolling down will zoom out. While scrolling, the slider bar indicates the degree of zoom. The exact center of this bar is the original image (no zooming applied). You can easily go back to the original zoom size by pressing the Menu key and selecting Zoom All.

Rotate it

Want to view yourself upside down? Not really. But sometimes your pictures may be best viewed sideways or you're just so bored that you like to exercise your neck. While you're viewing an image in Picture, press the trackball and select Rotate. The image rotates 90 degrees clockwise. You can keep rotating the image by repeating the steps of pressing the trackball and selecting Rotate; each time you get an additional 90-degree clockwise rotation.

Turn it down or blast it off

Whether you're listening to music or watching a video, adjusting the volume is easy because your BlackBerry Pearl comes with dedicated volume keys. They're located on the top right side of the device. The top key (with the plus sign) turns the volume up, and the one below it (with the minus sign) turns the volume down.

Commonly used navigation

Whether you're viewing a picture, listening to music, or watching a video clip, you can easily jump forward or backward to the next

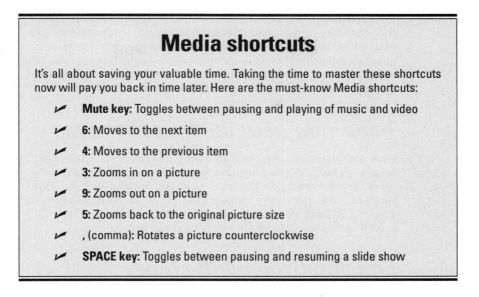

Media shortcuts

It's all about saving your valuable time. Taking the time to master these shortcuts now will pay you back in time later. Here are the must-know Media shortcuts:

- **Mute key:** Toggles between pausing and playing of music and video
- **6:** Moves to the next item
- **4:** Moves to the previous item
- **3:** Zooms in on a picture
- **9:** Zooms out on a picture
- **5:** Zooms back to the original picture size
- **, (comma):** Rotates a picture counterclockwise
- **SPACE key:** Toggles between pausing and resuming a slide show

item in the list. Press the Menu key while viewing a picture and you should see the following menu items:

- **Next:** Jumps to the next item in the list. This item appears only if there's an item next to this media file in the current folder.
- **Previous:** Jumps to the previous item. This item appears only if there's a previous item in the current folder.
- **Delete:** Deletes the media file.
- **Move:** Moves the file to a different folder.
- **Rename:** Renames the media file.
- **Properties:** Displays a screen showing the location of the media file, its size, and the time it was last modified.

Working with Media Files

Are you always on top of the new gizmo trends? Nowadays, methods of acquiring media files are evolving. Ten years back, who would think that we'd be buying music on a tiny SD card from Best Buy or downloading music from an "all you can" type monthly subscription.

Sure, technologies are exciting, but most of us are happy maintaining a music collection in one form or another, be it CDs or a digital format in our computer. Someday, we'll wake up with a technology that doesn't require us to deal with constantly copying media files from this collection to our handheld music players. But for now, enjoying music while on the move means managing these files. Media is a great music player, but without music files it's as useless as a guitar without strings. Enough with chitchat, let's get on with it.

Importing your media collection

First and foremost, you need to have a media collection in a digital format. In fact we'll just assume that you have that already. (A quick Web browsing on the topic of music burning will get your feet wet.) You can easily transfer that collection of media files to your BlackBerry Pearl. But wait a second; we have this topic covered in detail in Chapter 13, so check it out there.

Synchronizing with iTunes

If you have an iPod, it's likely that you are using iTunes and maintaining a playlist and perhaps a subscription to podcasts. Would you like to sync your BlackBerry with iTunes? Well, don't we all. Unfortunately, this is not done out of the box. After all, iTunes is not a RIM product. However, you can buy software called PearlTunes (http://pocketmac.net) for only $9.95, as of this writing.

Sharing media files using Bluetooth

We love sharing, especially if we're on the receiving end, right? You can send your media files to any Bluetooth-capable device. Here's how:

1. **From the Media screen, select the media type.**

2. **Select a media folder.**

   You may have to drill down to the folder to find the media file you're looking for.

3. **Press the Menu key and select Send Using Bluetooth.**

   At this point, Bluetooth displays all the paired Bluetooth devices. (Refer to Chapter 10 for more on Bluetooth enabling and pairing devices.)

4. **Select the Bluetooth-enabled device.**

5. **Select Send.**

   BlackBerry starts sending the file.

Downloading tunes

RIM has set up a Web site where you can download new ringtones. Simply point the Browser to the following and you'll get a screen similar to the one shown in Figure 12-4:

```
http://mobile.blackberry.com/mss/ringtone_catalog
```

From this page, you can sample and download alarms, notifiers, and tunes. And did we mention that it's free?

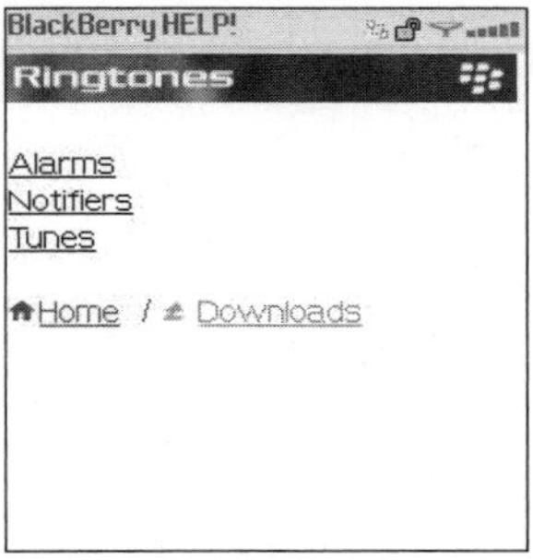

Figure 12-4: Download media files here.

Just select the tone you want from the three categories and it will begin playing. After the tune plays, you can save it by pressing the Menu key and selecting Save. RIM isn't the only site where you can find ringtones. The Web is a wonderful place, so go hunting.

Part IV
Working with Desktop Manager

Of course it doesn't make any sense, but it's our only chance! Now hook the BlackBerry Pearl into the override and see if you can bring this baby in.

In this part . . .

*H*ere, you discover essential information about some behind-the-scenes yet integral processes. Read all about Desktop Manager, which you direct to monitor and control database synchronization (Chapter 13), backing up your data (Chapter 14), and using your Pearl as a portable flash drive (Chapter 15).

Chapter 13

Synching the Synchronize Way

*W*hat better way to keep your BlackBerry Pearl updated than to synchronize it with your desktop application's data? Arguably, most of the data you need to synchronize is from your PIM (personal information manager) applications. PIM info includes notes, appointments, addresses, and tasks. The crucial piece for data synchronization to and from your device and desktop computer is the Synchronize software. Synchronize is a product of Puma Technologies, licensed by RIM to work inside BlackBerry Desktop Manager. This software allows you to synchronize your PIM data. But that's not all; it also lets you upload and download media files between your PC and Pearl.

In this chapter, we introduce Synchronize and show you how to manually and automatically synchronize your Pearl with your desktop computer. We also offer tips on which data synchronization options you might want to use. Before we get into all that, however, we include a section on the BlackBerry Desktop Manager.

Introduction to BlackBerry Desktop Manager

The centerpiece of the desktop activities you can do for your BlackBerry is the *BlackBerry Desktop Manager* (BDM), which is a suite of programs that include

- ✔ **Application Loader:** Installs BlackBerry applications and updates the BlackBerry OS (not covered in this book).

- ✔ **Backup and Restore:** Backs up your BlackBerry data and settings. Check Chapter 14 for details.

- ✔ **Synchronize:** Synchronizes your BlackBerry data to your PC (the topic of this chapter).

- ✔ **Media Manager:** Uploads media files on to your BlackBerry from your PC and vice versa (the topic of this chapter).

BDM is the software included on the CD that comes with your handheld device. Your BlackBerry's packaging provides instructions on how to install BDM on your desktop computer.

Launching BDM

In most Windows installations, you find the shortcut to launch BDM through the Start menu of your computer; choose Start➪ All Programs➪BlackBerry➪Desktop Manager. Connect your BlackBerry to your desktop computer using the USB cable that came with your device and then launch BDM. The BDM opening screen appears (see Figure 13-1).

Figure 13-1: The BlackBerry Desktop Manager.

Notice the number of icons on this screen. Each icon is an application by itself. Because BDM is a separate application, its installation might vary depending on the phone provider. At the very least, you should have at least three icons or three applications: Application Loader, Backup and Restore (Chapter 14), and Synchronize.

Connecting BDM to your Pearl

You establish a connection between your BlackBerry Pearl and the BDM through the USB cable that comes with your device. Plug in your device to your desktop. After BDM is running, it will try to find a BlackBerry on the type of connection specified. The default connection is USB, so it should work without your needing to configure anything.

If your device has a password, enter it at the prompt. You should then see Connected as the heading of the screen. If you see Disconnected and no password prompt, either BDM can't find the device being connected via USB or the connection setting is not set to use USB.

To make sure that the connection setting uses USB, do the following. From the BDM screen, choose Options⇨Connection Settings. The screen shown in Figure 13-2 appears. In the Connection drop-down list, select the USB connection that has the PIN of your BlackBerry.

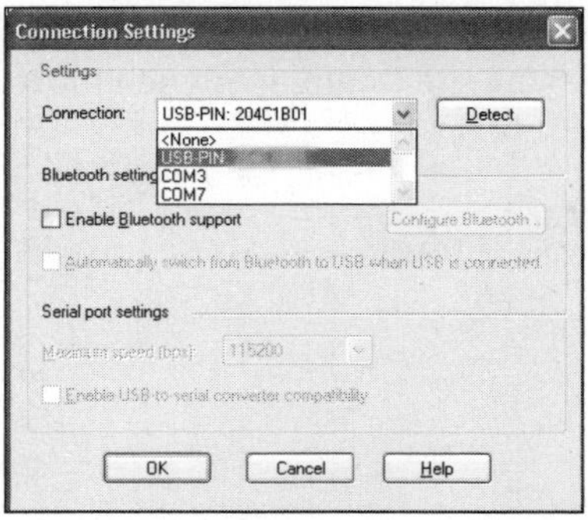

Figure 13-2: Possible connection types to your BlackBerry.

Setting Up Synchronize

Synchronize is the part of BDM that allows you to synchronize your data between your desktop computer and your Pearl. To launch Synchronize, simply double-click the Synchronize icon. A screen appears containing two tabs, as shown in Figure 13-3.

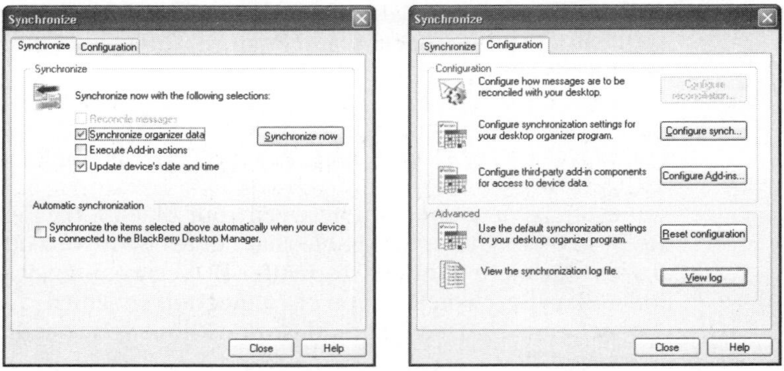

Figure 13-3: The Synchronize tab (left) and the Configuration tab (right).

The Synchronize tab allows you to manually trigger synchronization, and the Configure tab is where you can set up the configuration and rules for reconciling data. The first thing you need to figure out is the Configuration tab.

Configuring PIM synchronization

One important item in the Configuration tab is the Configure Synch button, where you can configure PIM (personal information manager) synchronization. PIM info includes notes, appointments, addresses, and tasks. Clicking the Configure Synch button displays the screen shown in Figure 13-4.

Figure 13-4: Configuring PIM info.

This screen is the entry point of the entire synchronization configuration for applications that are part of PIM. As you can see in Figure 13-4, the PIM handheld application is paired with a desktop application. This figure shows Outlook as the desktop application.

TIP

If you're curious as to what other applications the PIM Configuration option supports, click the Choose button. A screen similar to Figure 13-5 appears, which lists other possible applications. The list depends on the context of the highlighted PIM application. These other desktop applications are also popular; you're likely using one of them. Isn't it nice to know that you don't have to dump the application you're already familiar with?

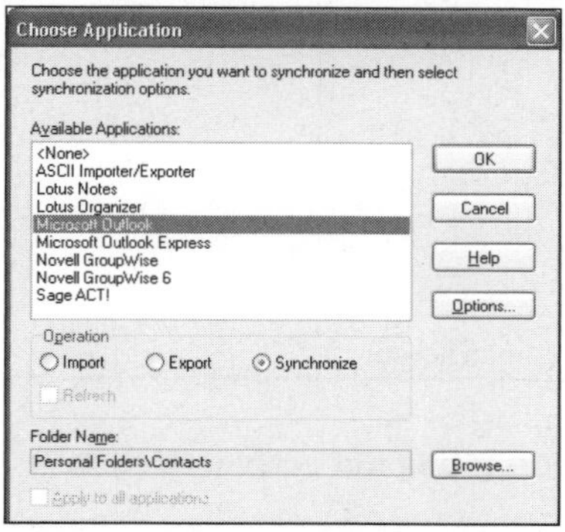

Figure 13-5: Other desktop apps that Synchronize supports for Address Book sync.

Confirming record changes

Face facts: Doing a desktop synchronization is not an interesting task, and not many people perform it on a regular basis. If you're one of those folks, you won't have any clue what changes to expect on either side. Well, not to worry. You can tell Synchronize to prompt you for any changes it's trying to do or perhaps undo on either side of the wire. This is where the Advanced Settings screen comes in. To get to this view, follow these steps:

1. **From BDM, double-click Synchronize.**

2. **From the Configuration screen that appears, click the Configure Synch button.**

   The PIM configuration screen appears (refer to Figure 13-4). At this point, Address Book is highlighted, so the next step is based on the Address Book application. If you want to go to the Confirmation tab of a PIM application other than Address Book, you have to click that application from the list at this point.

3. **Click the Configure button.**

4. Choose Advanced Settings from the drop-down list.

The Advanced Settings for Address Book screen appears, as shown in Figure 13-6. Note the Confirmation tab.

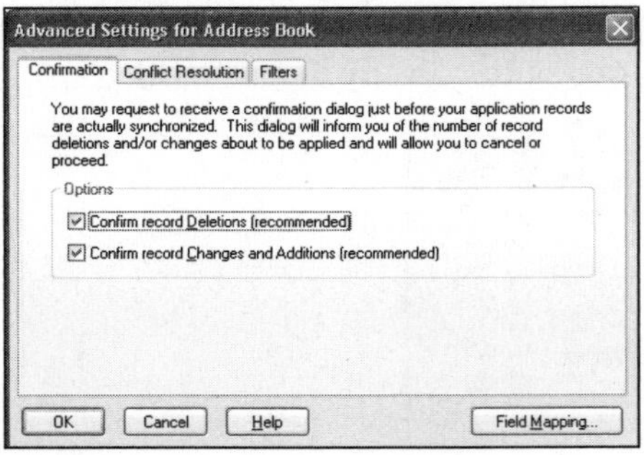

Figure 13-6: The Advanced Settings screen.

5. If the Confirmation tab is not active, click it.

You have the following options: You can display a prompt screen to confirm deletions, you can display a prompt screen to confirm updates and additions, or you can select both options.

6. Click the options you want, and then click OK to save the settings.

Regardless of whether you select the first option, Synchronize displays a prompt to confirm the deletion of all records.

Resolving update conflicts

If you don't synchronize your device frequently, you will get into a situation where you must make an update to a particular record on your BlackBerry as well as on your desktop application. Synchronize needs to know how you want this handled. The interface to define how to resolve these conflicts is the same for all PIM applications. Again, for illustration, we'll use the Address Book:

1. From BDM, double-click Synchronize.

2. From the Configuration screen that appears, click the Configure Synch button.

The PIM configuration screen appears (refer to Figure 13-4).

3. Click the Configure button.

4. **From the drop-down list that appears, choose Advanced Settings.**

   The Advanced Settings for Address Book screen appears (refer to Figure 13-6).

5. **Click the Conflict Resolution tab.**

   The Conflict Resolution tab comes into view, as shown in Figure 13-7.

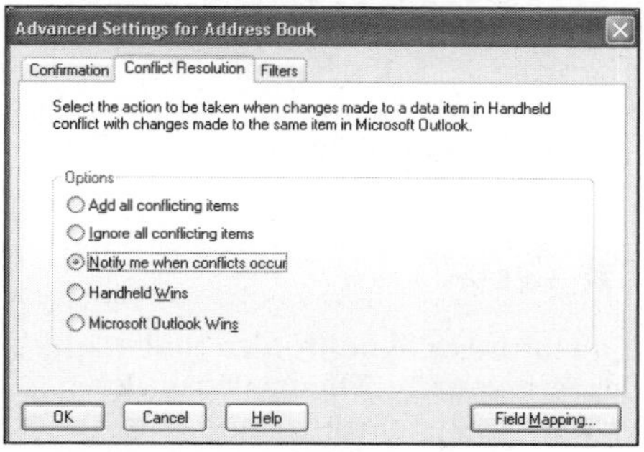

Figure 13-7: Manage conflicts here.

You can tell Synchronize to handle conflicts in several ways. Here are the options shown in the Address Book Advanced Setting screen:

- *Add All Conflicting Items:* When a conflict happens, add a new record to the BlackBerry for the changes done on the desktop, and add a new record to the desktop side for the changes done on the BlackBerry.

- *Ignore All Conflicting Items:* Ignore the fact that there has been a change to the record and keep the data the same on both sides.

- *Notify Me When Conflicts Occur:* This is the safest among the options. Synchronize displays a message screen with the details of the record that has a conflict and gives you the ability to resolve the conflict.

- *Handheld Wins:* Unless you are sure that this is the case, you shouldn't choose this option. It basically tells Synchronize to disregard the changes done in the desktop application and use handheld changes every time it encounters a conflict.

- Application *Wins:* The name of this option changes based on the application you're using. It's the opposite of the Handheld Wins option in that it tells Synchronize to always discard changes on the handheld and use the desktop application change whenever it encounters a conflict. Again, we don't recommend this option because there's no telling on which side you made the good update.

6. **Click the option you want and then click OK to save the settings.**

Ready, Set, Synchronize!

Are you ready to synchronize? Good. It's now time to be brave and push the button. Your two choices are manually (by using the Synchronize Now button) or automatically.

Synchronize Now

Synchronize Now is a feature of Synchronize that enables you to run the synchronization manually. The basic rundown is that you choose the data you want to synchronize and click the Synchronize Now button. That's it. Without delay, here are the steps:

1. **From BDM, double-click Synchronize.**

   The Synchronize screen appears (refer to the left screen in Figure 13-3). The four upper check boxes give you the option to selectively synchronize your data. You can choose from organizer data (such as calendar and Address Book), add-in, and date and time.

   Usually you have to make sure the Execute Add-in Action option is selected to sync with third-party applications. If you don't have a third-party application installed for your BlackBerry Pearl, you don't have to worry about this.

2. **Select the check boxes of the data you want to synchronize.**

   If you have automatic synchronization turned on (see the next section), the items you check here are automatically synched every time you connect your BlackBerry Pearl to your PC.

3. **Click the Synchronize Now button.**

   Synchronize starts running the synchronization; you see a progress screen. If you set up rules to prompt for conflicts and if Synchronize encounters one, you see a screen to resolve it. After synchronization is finished, the progress screen disappears, and the Synchronize screen returns.

4. **Close Synchronize by clicking the Close button.**

Automatic synchronization

How many times do you think you reconfigure your Synchronize setup? Rarely, right? After you have it configured, that's it. Yes, maybe once in a while you'll find a reason to change something, but it's mostly static. And if you're like us, the reason you open BlackBerry Desktop Manager is because you want to run Synchronize. So, opening Synchronize and clicking the Synchronize Now button is annoying.

If you'd like to make Synchronize run automatically every time you connect your BlackBerry Pearl to your PC, simply select the last check box in the Synchronize tab (Synchronize the Items Selected). You might be asking, "What items will the auto-synchronization synch?" Good question. It will auto-synch the items you've checked in the top portion of the Synchronization tab. Simple. (Refer to the left screen in Figure 13-3 for the Synchronization tab.)

Managing Your Media on Your Pearl

With the BlackBerry Desktop Manager (BDM), you can transfer media files between your Pearl and your PC. It's quite simple.

Media Manager allows you to transfer files only to your Pearl's internal memory, not to the memory in your microSD card. (A microSD card allows you to store more files on your BlackBerry Pearl. See Chapter 16 for where you can purchase one.)

If you want to carry a few pictures of your loved on your Pearl, you can simply do the following:

1. **Use a USB cable to connect your Pearl to your PC.**

2. **From BDM, double-click Media Manager.**

   The Media Manager screen appears, as shown in Figure 13-8. The left side of the screen shows files on your PC, and the right side of the screen shows files on your Pearl.

3. **On the left side of the screen, highlight the files you want to transfer from your PC.**

   We assume that you know where to look for the files that you want to transfer.

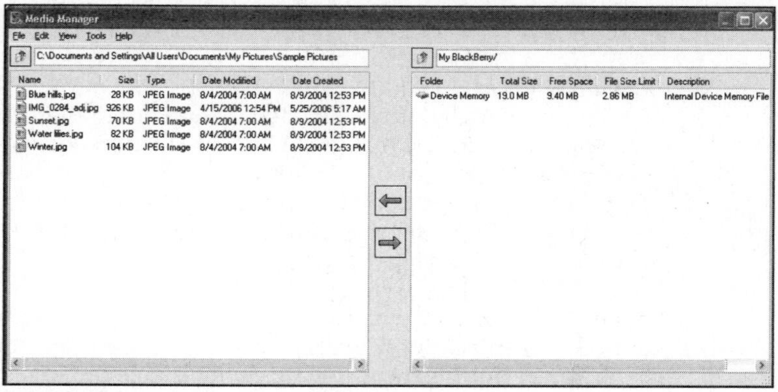

Figure 13-8: The Media Manager screen.

4. On the right side of the screen, select the destination folder where you want your files to be stored on your BlackBerry Pearl.

5. Click the right arrow.

The right arrow transfers files from your PC to your Pearl.

Make sure that the files you're transferring are small enough to fit into your Pearl's internal memory. You can check how much free memory you have on the right side of the Media Manager screen.

To transfer files to your PC from your Pearl, click the left arrow instead of the right arrow in Step 5.

Chapter 14

Protecting Your Information

● ●

In This Chapter

▶ Performing a full backup of your BlackBerry information

▶ Scheduling automatic backups

▶ Restoring from backups

▶ Selectively backing up information

● ●

*I*magine that you left your BlackBerry Pearl in the back of a cab or on the train. You've lost your Pearl for good. Okay, not good. So what happens to all your information? Have you lost it forever? What about information security? Can anyone have unauthorized access to your personal information?

One thing that you *don't* need to worry about is information security — assuming that you set up a security password on your BlackBerry. With security password protection, anyone who finds your BlackBerry has only ten chances to enter the correct password; after those ten chances are up, it's self-destruction time. Although it's not as smoky and dramatic as what you see on *Mission Impossible,* your BlackBerry does erase all its information in such a scenario, thwarting your would-be data thief. Therefore, set up a password for your BlackBerry! For information on how to do so, refer to Chapter 3.

What you *do* need to worry about is how to get back all your information on your BlackBerry Pearl. If you're like us and you store important information on your Pearl, this chapter is for you. Vital information such as clients' and friends' contact information, notes from phone calls with clients — and, of course, those precious e-mail messages — should not be taken lightly. Backing up this information is a reliable way to protect information from being lost forever.

In this chapter, we show you how you can prevent losing information on your BlackBerry by backing that information up on your PC. Then we show you how to restore and recover the information you've backed up.

Accessing Backup and Restore

Backup and Restore is a mini-application within the BlackBerry Desktop Manager (BDM). For instructions on installing BDM, see Chapter 13. After BlackBerry Desktop Manager is installed on your PC, you can connect your BlackBerry to your PC by using the USB cable that comes with your BlackBerry. If everything is set up properly, you see a pop-up window on your PC prompting you to type your BlackBerry security password. After you enter your correct password, the BlackBerry is connected to the PC.

To access Backup and Restore, double-click the Backup and Restore icon on the BlackBerry Desktop Manager screen. Doing so opens the Backup and Restore screen (see Figure 14-1). From this point, you're ready to back up or restore information from or to your BlackBerry.

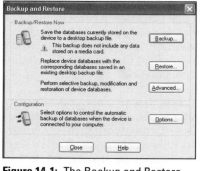

Figure 14-1: The Backup and Restore screen.

Backing Up BlackBerry Style

We all know that backing up your data provides tremendous peace of mind when protecting your data. So do the folks at RIM, which is why they made backing up your information quite easy. Your Pearl can be backed up manually or by autopilot.

Backing up your BlackBerry manually

To back up your BlackBerry manually:

1. **From the BDM screen, double-click the Backup and Restore icon.**

   The Back and Restore screen appears (refer to Figure 14-1).

2. **Click the Backup button.**

   The dialog box shown in Figure 14-2 appears, so you can name the backup file and determine where you want it saved on your PC.

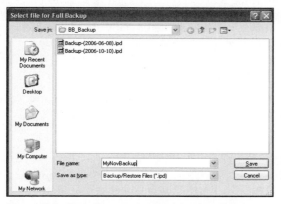

Figure 14-2: Set where to save your backup file.

3. **Name your backup file, choose a place to save it, and then click Save.**

   BlackBerry Desktop Manager automatically starts backing up your BlackBerry information onto your PC. You can follow the backup progress from the Transfer In Progress window that appears (see Figure 14-3).

Figure 14-3: A backup is in progress.

Do not unplug your BlackBerry from the PC until the backup process finishes! Depending on how much information you have on your BlackBerry, the backup might take five to ten minutes to finish.

4. **When the Transfer In Progress window disappears, you are finished with the BlackBerry backup process and may unplug the Pearl from the PC.**

Setting up automatic backups

What is better than backing up your information once? Remembering to back up regularly! What's better than regularly backing up? You guessed it — having your PC and BlackBerry run backups automatically. After you schedule automated backups of your BlackBerry, you can really have peace of mind when it comes to preventing information loss.

To set up an autobackup:

1. **From the BDM, double-click the Backup and Restore icon.**

   The Backup and Restore screen appears (refer to Figure 14-1).

2. **Click the Options button.**

   The Backup and Restore Options screen appears, as shown in Figure 14-4, where you can schedule automatic backups.

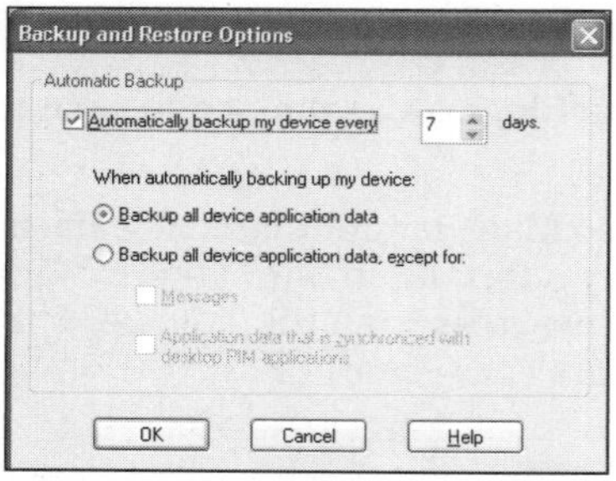

Figure 14-4: Set autobackups here.

3. **Enable the Automatically Backup My Device Every option.**

   This enables you to configure more options (check boxes and options become active), such as how often Desktop Manager should back up your BlackBerry.

4. **Select the number of days, between 1 and 99, in the numeric Days field.**

   This interval sets how often your BlackBerry will be backed up. For example, if you enter 14 days, your BlackBerry will be backed up every 14 days.

5. **In the When Automatically Backing Up My Device section, select the Backup All Device Application Data option.**

   This backs up all the data on your Pearl each time auto-backup runs.

   Although you have the option to exclude e-mail messages and information, such as from Address Book, to-do's, and memos, we recommend that you back up everything each time without any exclusion.

6. **Confirm your settings by clicking OK.**

   Now you can go on with your life without caring too much about backing up information on your BlackBerry.

To run a back up, you need to connect your BlackBerry Pearl to your PC. Thus, if you travel often or just don't link your BlackBerry to your PC often, make sure you plug your Pearl into your PC once in a while so the autobackup has a chance to back up your information.

Full Restore from Backup Information

We hope that you never have to read this section more than once because every time you perform a full restore from backup, it probably means that you've lost information that you hope to find from the backup you created on your PC.

The steps to fully restoring your backup information are simple:

1. **From the BDM, double-click the Backup and Restore icon.**

   The Backup and Restore screen appears.

2. **Click the Restore button.**

   Doing so brings up a typical Open file dialog box, asking you where the backup file is located on your PC.

3. **Choose a backup file and then click Open.**

   A Warning window appears (see Figure 14-5) alerting you that you're about to overwrite existing information.

4. **From this Warning window, click OK to proceed with the full restore.**

   A progress bar similar to Figure 14-3 now appears, showing progress of the full restore. When the progress bar disappears, your BlackBerry Pearl is now fully restored from the backup file.

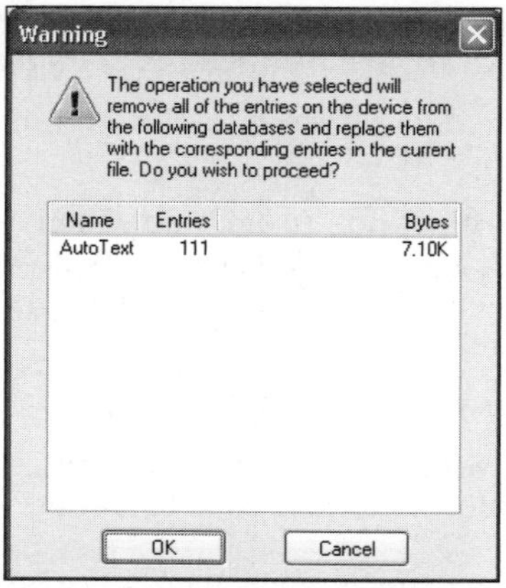

Warning

The operation you have selected will remove all of the entries on the device from the following databases and replace them with the corresponding entries in the current file. Do you wish to proceed?

Name	Entries	Bytes
AutoText	111	7.10K

OK   Cancel

Figure 14-5: Take caution when overwriting existing info.

It might take awhile for the full restore to finish. Do not unplug your Pearl from your PC during this time!

5. **When the progress bar disappears, you're finished with the restore process and may unplug the Pearl from the PC.**

Protecting Your Data, Your Way

A certain burger joint and BlackBerry Pearl have in common that you can have it *your way* with their products. Just like you can get your burger with or without all the extras (such as pickles and onions), you can choose to not backup and restore things that you know you won't need.

For example, say you've accidentally deleted all your Browser bookmarks and now you want them back. The thing *not* to do is to restore all the information from your last backup, which could potentially be more than 90 days old (depending on how often your autobackup runs, if it does). Doing so might overwrite other information, such as e-mail or your Address Book contacts. The easiest thing to do is use the selective backup/restore function on the BlackBerry Desktop Manager and to restore *only* Browser bookmarks.

The same idea goes with backing up. If you are a big e-mail user and your mailbox is constantly growing, you can choose to back up just your e-mails and nothing else.

In this section, we use the term *databases*. Don't worry; this isn't as technical as you think. Think of a database as an information category on the BlackBerry Pearl. For example, saying, "backing up your Browser bookmarks database" is just a fancy way of saying, "backing up all your Browser bookmarks on your Pearl."

We start with selective backup and then go over restoring selectively.

Backing up, your way

To show you how to perform selective backups, we'll back up just e-mails and Browser bookmarks.

To back up selectively, follow these steps:

1. **From the BDM, double-click the Backup and Restore icon.**

   The Backup and Restore screen appears (refer to Figure 14-1).

2. **Click the Advanced button.**

   The advanced Backup/Restore screen appears, as shown in Figure 14-6. On the right side of the screen are the different information categories, or *databases,* of your BlackBerry.

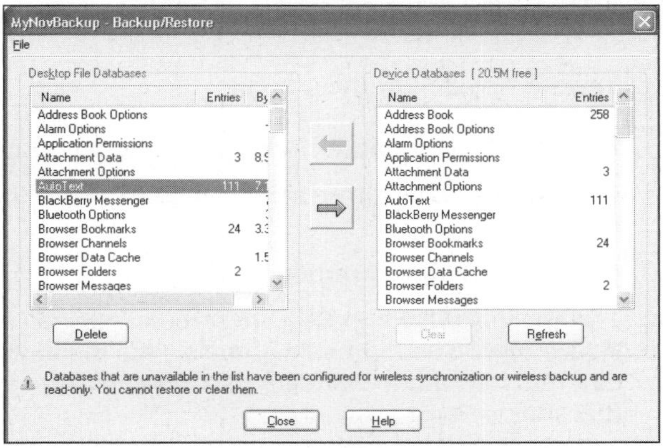

Figure 14-6: The advanced Backup/Restore screen.

3. **Ctrl+click Browser Bookmarks and Browser Messages (from the right side of the screen) as the databases you want to back up. Then click the left-facing arrow (the Backup arrow).**

A progress bar moves while your BlackBerry is backed up selectively. This step merely transfers the databases onto your PC; it does not save them. When the backup transfer is finished, you can see the two databases on the left side of the window.

4. **Choose File⟹Save As.**

5. **Name your file and specify where you want to save it on your PC.**

You still need to manually save the backup file on your PC even after you choose a location for the file in Step 3. A selective backup does not automatically save your backup on your PC.

Restoring, your way

Selective restoring works in a similar way to a selective backup. However, when restoring, you need to already have a backup file to restore from. Although this might sound obvious to you, the point we are making is that you can selectively restore from any backup, auto or manual. For example, say you have autobackup running every other day, and you want to restore only your e-mail messages from two days ago. You don't need to do a full restore because that might overwrite some of the new contacts in your Address Book. Rather, you can use the selective restoring method and get back only your e-mail messages.

To restore your way, follow these steps:

1. **From the BDM, double-click the Backup and Restore icon.**

   The Backup and Restore screen appears (refer to Figure 14-1).

2. **Click the Advanced button.**

   The advanced Backup/Restore screen appears (refer to Figure 14-6). The right side of the screen displays the different information categories, or *databases*, of your BlackBerry Pearl.

3. **Choose File⟹Open.**

   This opens a window where you can choose which backup file you want to restore from.

   A BlackBerry backup file has an `.ipd` suffix.

4. **Select a backup file and then click the Open button.**

The different information categories, or databases, appear on the left side of the screen. You are now ready for a selective restore.

5. **Select the categories, or databases, of your choice.**

   You can select multiple databases by Ctrl+clicking the databases you want.

6. **Click the right-facing arrow (the Restore arrow).**

   You will likely see a Warning window asking whether you want to replace all the information with the data you are restoring (refer to Figure 14-5).

   If your Pearl has the same categories as the ones you are restoring (which is likely), you will overwrite any information you have on your Pearl.

   You can confidently click OK if you know that the database you're restoring has the information you're looking for.

7. **From the Warning window, click OK.**

   A progress bar similar to the one in Figure 14-3 appears while the selective restore is in progress. When the progress bar window disappears, the information categories that you've selected are restored on your BlackBerry.

Clearing BlackBerry information, your way

You can also clear, or delete, information on your BlackBerry selectively from the BlackBerry Desktop Manager. And when would you use selective deletion? Suppose you want to clear only your phone logs from your BlackBerry. One way is to tediously select one phone log at a time and press Delete, and then repeat that until all phone logs are deleted. However, a faster way is to use selective deleting. The idea is to delete a database from the advanced Backup/Restore screen by using the Backup and Restore function of the BlackBerry Desktop Manager.

To selectively delete databases on your BlackBerry, follow these steps:

1. **From the BDM, double-click the Backup and Restore icon.**

   The Backup and Restore screen appears (refer to Figure 14-1).

2. **Click the Advanced button.**

   The advanced Backup/Restore screen appears (refer to Figure 14-6). The right side of the screen displays the different information categories, or databases, of your BlackBerry Pearl.

3. **Ctrl+click the database(s) you want to delete.**

   This highlights the database(s).

4. **Click the Clear button on the right side of the screen.**

   A Warning window appears, asking you to confirm your deletion.

5. **Click OK.**

   A progress bar appears, showing the progress of the deletion. When the progress bar disappears, the information categories you selected are cleared from your BlackBerry.

Chapter 15

Using Your Pearl as a Portable Flash Drive

*F*irst off the bat, what is a media card? A media card is not what you use to gain privileged access to some event, "Let me in, I'm CNN." No, far from that. How about flash drive? It's not your neighbor's driveway that looks like a runway with those perfectly aligned solar lights.

Okay, a *flash drive* contains a flash memory card and a card reader. The drive is a tiny removable component commonly used in hand-held devices, such as digital cameras, to store memory. It is typically lightweight and both readable and writable.

Several types of flash memory cards are available, but in BlackBerry Pearl land, you need to use a microSD (a flash memory card originally manufactured by Sandisk), which the Pearl folks refers to as a media card. You don't need a reader because BlackBerry Pearl itself can read the card directly. As of this writing, you can avail yourself of microSD cards in capacities from 128MB through 2GB. Capacities are growing fast, so by the time this book is published, it's conceivable that you might be seeing 4GB to 100GB. (Nah, the last number mentioned is our wish.)

Feeling lost with all these media files located in multiple devices? Whether its picture files, music files, or video files, it doesn't matter. They seem to be everywhere nowadays, and it's maddening when you can't find the one you need the moment you need it. Some of the more organized folks among us try to manage files (any files) by having a copy in a central location. And this location is usually the desktop computer. No wonder RIM made a point to make Pearl connect seamlessly with your PC. With a USB connection, Pearl automatically becomes a virtual drive in your desktop computer. Once connected, you can use your BlackBerry with a media card to back up your files to your computer or to copy a file from your library. What you do with this new portable drive is beyond us, but this chapter shows you the tricks. This chapter also describes the details of the Media Card.

The Media Card

What BlackBerry Pearl calls a *media card* is a tiny microSD. How tiny is tiny? Just take a look at the left image in Figure 15-1. It's a microSD on top of a postage stamp. The microSD barely covers half the stamp.

Figure 15-1: The tiny media card (left); inserting media card here (right).

Acquiring one

When you recently purchased your BlackBerry Pearl, it's likely that it didn't come with a microSD card. But with a little cash, you can get a decent capacity card from the Web, from a computer store, from an electronic store such as Best Buy or Circuit City, or even at a big discount warehouse such as Costco.

What to buy? The bigger the capacity, the better. Any particular brands? Well, microSD is originally based on Sandisk's Transflash card format. So, getting a Sandisk brand is your safest bet, but you pay a little premium compared to other brands. To get more information on other brands, Google *microSD reviews*.

Inserting the card

If you want to use a media card, you need to insert it in the back of the device. Refer to the right of Figure 15-1 for the exact location. You have to take off the cover, remove the battery, and slide the metal slot slightly to the left using your thumb. You should be able to tilt the slot up and insert the card. Make sure that the metal portion of the card is facing down. Push down the metal slot with the card in it and slide it slightly back to the right. The slot should snugly fit back in place. Put back the battery and slide back the cover and you're on your way to enjoying a bigger media memory storage.

Formatting the card

When you first insert a new media card to your BlackBerry Pearl, the card might not be formatted, so your device may not be able to use it. No worries, you can easily format the card and things will go smoothly after that.

Follow these steps to format your media:

1. **From the Home screen, press the Menu key and select Security Options.**

2. **Select Advanced Options and then select Media Card.**

   The Media Card screen appears, as shown in Figure 15-2.

Media Card	
Media Card Support:	On
Encryption Mode:	
	Security Password
Encrypt Media Files:	Yes
Mass Storage Mode Support:	On
Auto Enable Mass Storage Mode When Connected:	
	Prompt
Total Space:	31.94MB
Free Space:	31.93MB

Figure 15-2: Set your Media Card options here.

3. **Press the Menu key and select Format Card.**

   A screen shows up, warning you that any content on this card will be wiped and lost.

4. **Select Yes.**

Your media card is now formatted.

Formatting a media card means wiping clean all its contents. If you've used this media card before and have files in it, say goodbye to them.

To figure out the total amount of space as well as the free space on your media card, you can find it in the Media Card screen (refer to Figure 15-2).

Setting to mass storage mode

Mass storage mode means allowing your BlackBerry Pearl to behave as a PC flash drive. You can keep it enabled, but the default is Prompt, as shown in Figure 15-2. Prompt means whenever you connect the BlackBerry Pearl to your PC, the device will prompt to enable mass storage mode.

So, if you want your device to become a flash drive, always make sure that you answer Yes on the prompt or you can set it to always on by going to the Media screen as described in Steps 1 and 2 in the preceding section. In the Media screen, highlight the Auto Enable Mass Storage Mode field, press the trackball, and select Yes. Then press the Menu key and select Save.

Copying Files between the PC and Pearl

The easy part is connecting the Pearl to the PC — even a six-year-old can do this. All you need is your BlackBerry Pearl, your desktop computer, and the USB cable that came with your device. When talking about a desktop computer, we mean a PC running Windows 98, 2000, XP, or Vista. If you are a Mac user, please refer to our companion Web site for details on how to copy files between your Mac and Pearl:

```
www.blackberryfordummies.com/pearl
```

Connect the PC and your BlackBerry Pearl using the USB cable, and your computer should detect the device and display a screen similar to Figure 15-3. You can choose from any of the options in this screen.

Figure 15-3: Choose what you do with your flash drive here.

For example, to copy a file, select Open Folder to View Files. This opens the familiar Windows Explorer screen, as shown in Figure 15-4. After you get to this screen, you basically can do anything you do with a normal Windows folder. You can drag and drop files, copy files, and delete files.

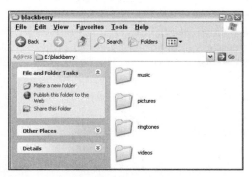

Figure 15-4: Your flash drive opens in a familiar Windows Explorer folder.

Securing Your Files

Most of the time, security is the last thing you think about when you're using a flash drive — although you might begin to become uneasy when you start copying sensitive information into the drive. We're not talking about embarrassing pictures; we're talking about information such as bank statements, tax statements, or employment contracts. Now, consider the statistics of cellphones left in taxi cabs and your mind begins to wonder about all the nasty possibilities. You don't have to go far with your imagination. Just relax because the good people at RIM are serious about security. Your device is capable of encrypting files stored in the media card.

You need to do two things to make sure that security is as tight as possible. One is to set a device password. This ensures that no one can take a look at what's inside your BlackBerry even if it falls in the wrong hands. And two, encrypt the files in your media card. This makes sure that if someone attempts to open the media card, it will ask for your secret password.

Setting a device password

You can set a secret password for your device that you'll be prompted to enter every time you try to open the Pearl. It's quite easy to do, just follow these steps:

1. **From the Home screen, press the Menu key and select Options.**

2. **Select Security Options and then select General Settings.**

3. **Highlight the Password field, press the trackball, and select Enabled.**

   Setting the Password field to Enabled requires you to enter a password each time you open your BlackBerry. After you save this setting, your BlackBerry Pearl will ask you for this password.

4. **Press the Menu key and select Save.**

   At this point, two screens shows up in succession; one to initially enter your password and the second one for you to confirm the password.

5. **Enter the password you want and press the trackball. Do the same for the confirmation screen.**

   Your device now requires you to enter a password.

Encrypting media files

Your BlackBerry offers three modes for encrypting files in your media card. Here's the rundown:

- ✔ **Device:** Your device generates an encryption key.

- ✔ **Security Password:** The files are encrypted using the device password you entered.

- ✔ **Security Password & Device:** The files are encrypted using the device password and a device-generated encryption key.

Encrypting your media files is easy, here's how:

1. **From the Home screen, press the Menu key and select Options.**

2. **Select Advanced Options and then select Media Card.**

   A Media Card screen appears, as shown in Figure 15-2. To encrypt your media files, you need to set the following values:

   - *Media Card Support:* On.
   - *Encryption Mode:* Device, Security Password, or Security Password & Device.
   - *Encrypt Media Files:* Yes.

3. **Press the Menu key and select Save.**

4. **If you choose an Encryption Mode of Security Password or Security Password & Device, respond to the two screens that appear in succession.**

   The first screen allows you to enter the Security Password and the second one confirms the password.

Just in case your memory fails you, the Password Keeper is always there. So, use it to store your media card password. Refer to Chapter 6 for more info on the Password Keeper.

If you choose to encrypt your media files, every time you connect your BlackBerry to a PC, it will ask for the password. The password prompt is in the device, not in the PC.

Part V
The Part of Tens

The 5th Wave   By Rich Tennant

"He seemed nice, but I could never connect with someone who had a ring tone like his."

In this part . . .

If the earlier parts of this book are the cake and frosting, this part is the cherry on top. Delve into these two short but sweet chapters to find out how to accessorize your BlackBerry and maximize your BlackBerry experience.

For more on the Part of Tens, please visit our Web site at

www.blackberryfordummies.com/pearl/ten/
index.html

Chapter 16

Ten Great BlackBerry Accessories

In This Chapter

▶ BlackBerry accessories you can't live without

▶ Where to buy them

*T*he BlackBerry retail box contains a few essentials: a battery, a charger, and a USB cable. If you're like us, though, you're not satisfied with just what's included in the box. In this chapter, we present the accessories that we think supplement your BlackBerry well and also where to shop for them.

For more on BlackBerry Pearl games and productivity programs, please check our companion Web site

`www.blackberryfordummies.com/pearl/ten/index.html`

Cases for Protection and Style

If your Pearl didn't come with a case (most don't), you need to get one so when you carry it around, it doesn't get scratched or damaged. Whether you like a sporty look or a professional look, here are a few recommendations. These cases will set you back anywhere from $20–$40, which isn't too bad for looking hip.

✔ BlackBerryDen.com:

`http://store.blackberryden.com/bluepearl.html`

✔ BlackBerryStuff.com:

`www.blackberrystuff.com/blackberry-8100-pearl-case-accessory.htm`

BlackBerry Screen Protector

If the protector case described in the preceding section is a bit stressful for your wallet, try Screenguardz, for only $12. Your screen will be scratchless with Screenguardz. You can get it from BlackberrySource.com, at

```
www.blackberrysource.com/store/catalog.asp?item=680
```

MicroSD Memory Card

If you want to store lots of music, pictures, or simply files on your BlackBerry Pearl, you definitely need to get a microSD memory card. Depending on your needs, microSD memory capacity ranges from 32MB to 2GB. You can get a card from almost all the online shops. Here are just a couple places to get you started:

- ✔ Amazon.com:

    www.amazon.com/SanDisk-MicroSD-Card-Retail-Package/dp/B000EEZCEG/sr=8-1/qid=1162737636/ref=pd_bbs_sr_1/102-7738096-2386528?ie=UTF8&s=electronics

- ✔ Buy.com:

    www.buy.com/retail/product.asp?loc=101&sku =202611635

 If your laptop comes with an SD slot, make sure to buy a microSD card that comes with a card adapter. That way, you can use the same microSD card for your laptop. Two uses for the price of one. Nice!

Long Live Your BlackBerry

An extra battery for your BlackBerry will come in handy if you're a daily BlackBerry user. We recommend that you buy your battery only from Research in Motion (RIM), the maker of BlackBerry, and not from some other manufacturer because a faulty battery can seriously damage your BlackBerry beyond repair.

You can buy a battery manufactured by RIM from

- ✔ Shopblackberry.com:

    www.shopblackberry.com.

- ✔ BlackBerryStuff.com:

    www.blackberrystuff.com/blackberry-8100-pearl-battery-accessory.htm

Replenishing Your BlackBerry

If you're always on the go, you better have a portable charger on hand. The charger included with your BlackBerry is great to carry around town (and the world) because it has multiple adapters for different countries' electric plugs. The one we recommend is the BlackBerry Car Charger, which is great for all you road warriors out there. It will set you back around $30. Get your car charger from the official RIM online shopping store: www.shopblackberry.com.

Make sure that the charger you buy is for your BlackBerry model.

Bluetooth Hands-Free Headset

If you're a frequent phone user, we definitely recommend that you pick up a Bluetooth hands-free headset. Even though a wired hands-free headset comes with your BlackBerry, the convenience of a wireless Bluetooth hands-free headset is hard to live without.

Plenty of Bluetooth headsets are on the market for you to choose from. Here is our short-list:

- Jabra BT150
- Motorola HS850, H700, or H500
- Plantronics Explorer 320 or Voyager 510

When choosing a headset consider a comfortable fit, the voice quality, and whether it has a rechargeable battery.

You probably need to spend anywhere from $50–$100 for a hands-free headset. The best place to get your Bluetooth headset is good ol' Amazon.com: www.amazon.com.

Full Keyboard

If you compose long e-mails and draft long proposals on your BlackBerry, a full-sized keyboard is perfect for you. Not only will you save on typing time, but you will also save your thumbs from blistering.

You have your choice of Bluetooth and non-Bluetooth connection options.

✔ **Bluetooth:** At the time of writing, only one portal Bluetooth keyboard was available. We plan to offer more updates on this on our Web site, www.blackberryfordummies.com. For less than $100, you can own this cool Bluetooth keyboard. Not too bad for a wireless keyboard. Here's where to get the one that's available: eAccess Solutions, at www.eaccess-estore.com.

✔ **USB cable:** For about $200, you can get a USB cable keyboard. The price is a bit stiff, but depending on how you use your BlackBerry, it might be a good investment. Go to Man & Machine at www.man-machine.com/coolmir.htm.

External Speaker Phone

Even though some of you have a BlackBerry that comes with a speaker phone, sometimes the sound quality just isn't good enough for you to comprehend the phone conversation while in a car. Check out the wireless Bluetooth speaker phone, Blue Vision Bluetooth Speakerphone. For about $100, you can get it from BlackBerrySource.com:

    www.blackberrysource.com/store/catalog.asp?item=236

BlackBerry Car Mount

To complete your BlackBerry car experience, you need a place to mount your BlackBerry in your car. Enter the Auto PDA Holder Kit. For about $30, your BlackBerry will be securely fastened to the Auto PDA Holder so that your BlackBerry is in your sight at all times. You can get it from BlackberrySource.com:

    www.blackberrysource.com/store/catalog.asp?item=217

BlackBerry Pearl Cleaner

After you have your Pearl for more than a day, it's no longer clean and shiny. Instead, it's covered with fingerprints and smudges. The solution: Monster ScreenClean kit, which comes with a nonabrasive microfiber cloth. The ScreenClean kit work wonders not only on your BlackBerry Pearl but also on all types of surfaces — LCD, TV, and iPod. You can get it here:

    www.monstercable.com/productPage.asp?pin=2350

Chapter 17

Ten Must-Have BlackBerry Pearl Programs

In This Chapter

▶ Ten must-have applications for your BlackBerry Pearl

▶ Where to download these applications

*Y*our BlackBerry Pearl is a relatively new product, but BlackBerry has been with us for quite some time. And the industry of BlackBerry software is exploding at a dizzying rate. It's no longer easy to find out which of these applications are getting traction and hitting the mainstream user base, not to mention which ones are worth using. The ten applications we feature here are just the tip of the iceberg. By all means, feel free to surf the Internet because by the time this book is published, more software will likely be available. And don't forget to visit our Web site at

`www.blackberryfordummies.com/pearl/ten/index.html`

AskMeNow

Stop scratching your head. When you have a pressing question, you don't need to look for answers anywhere other than your BlackBerry Pearl. After you install the AskMeNow application, a guru is ready to answer that nagging question in your head. If your query can possibly be answered by a human being, you can ask it here. If you don't know what to ask, AskMeNow has precanned questions such as directions, weather, sports updates, and flight information. The answer is sent to you through e-mail, usually within two minutes. AskMeNow started as free, then became a fee service, but now it's back to being free again. We hope that when this book is published, the service will still be free. We've been using AskMeNow and we can tell you that it's great. For a free trial download, from your BlackBerry Pearl, go to

`www.blackberryfordummies.com/pearl/ten/ask.html`

BBToday

If you're experiencing information overload, you're not alone. BBToday helps you make sense of all this information without so much hair-pulling. In a nutshell, BBToday tries to give you a tearsheet on a daily basis. The nice thing about BBToday is its capability to show up every time you unlock or open your BlackBerry Pearl. It displays full screen with the following information in a summarized format:

- Current date and time
- E-mail summary
- Remaining battery strength
- Signal strength
- Appointments scheduled for the day
- Tasks scheduled for the day
- Current weather information and five-day forecast
- Phone call summary
- Stock quotes

This is like having an assistant tell you what your day will be like, organizing your PIM (personal information manager) information, and presenting it in such a way that you don't have to spend time viewing each of your PIM applications. You can configure the weather to point to your local area. You can also add the stock ticker for the stock quotes section. You can download BBToday for free from your BlackBerry Pearl by going to

```
www.blackberryfordummies.com/pearl/ten/bbtoday.html
```

English Language Acronyms Dictionary for BlackBerry 4.0

Your BlackBerry Pearl can be a good and reliable acronyms dictionary whenever you need one; just download English Language Acronyms Dictionary for BlackBerry 4.0. Of course, you could argue that you can use Browser and get a free dictionary from the Web, but this one works even when you're out of range. The software is easy to use and has more than 12,000 English acronyms. To download, go to

```
www.blackberryfordummies.com/pearl/ten/ea.html
```

This is another freebie, so there's no reason for not getting it.

Berry411

Here's another free program in your arsenal. Berry411 works the same as your local 411 information source, but you don't have to pay for the service. You get yellow as well as white pages. We found this useful for getting movie times for local movie theaters. If you're traveling, simply wise the address information of the hotel where you're staying, and Berry411 can get local information based on that address. To download, go to

```
www.blackberryfordummies.com/pearl/ten/b411.html
```

Handmark Pocket Express

The Handmark Pocket Express is a one-stop shop with a dizzying amount of information. You'll get the following features: 411 directory search, street maps, driving directions, movie showtimes, portfolio tracking, American writers, thesaurus, Dear Abby, Last Word in Astrology, News of the Weird, Scott Burns columns, NASCAR Insider, Motor Sports, and almost all categories of news. What's the catch? Not everything comes for free. To get the most out of it, you have to pay a subscription of $69.90 a year or $6.99 a month. From your PC or your BlackBerry Pearl Browser, go to

```
www.blackberryfordummies.com/pearl/ten/hpe.html
```

Stock Ticker

In the world of stock markets, timing is everything. For those who are actively trading — if you can't enjoy your latté without worrying about what's going on with your stocks — here is a piece of software that helps. Stock Ticker gives you the latest quotes and stock information, even when you're not looking at your three stock-monitor terminals. It features a scrolling interface with minute-by-minute news and commentaries. For about $50 a year, you can download Stock Ticker from your PC at

```
www.blackberryfordummies.com/pearl/ten/st.html
```

Wisespent Professional

Now, this is cool: expense tracker software, right on your handheld. The developers of Wisespent Professional listened to their customers and made many updates based on their feedback and requests. At the time of this writing, the software is version 3.0. What's nice about Wisespent is its support for importing data to popular expense software such as Quicken. For $23, you can download Wisespent Professional from your PC by going to

www.blackberryfordummies.com/pearl/ten/ws.html

trackIT: Vehicle Edition

Turn your BlackBerry Pearl into an extensive vehicle tracking system. The trackIT: Vehicle Edition software tracks maintenance, mileage, fuel, expenses, and more. It's loaded with features and easy to use. The price is $24.95, and you can download it to your PC by going to

www.blackberryfordummies.com/pearl/ten/trackit.html

Ascendo Fitness for BlackBerry

For the heath-conscious among us, here is award-winning software for your BlackBerry Pearl. Ascendo Fitness allows you to take control of your health by helping you track calories from what you eat and how you burn them in your exercise. It presents your progress using graphs. Based on your data, Ascendo calculators give you your ideal or healthy weight, your Body Mass Index (BMI), maximum heart rate based on age, and Basal Metabolism Ratio (BMR). We've heard many good comments from those who use this product. For $27, you can download Ascendo Fitness to your PC by going to

www.blackberryfordummies.com/pearl/ten/asc.html

4INFO Mobile

We haven't forgotten the sport fanatics among us. 4INFO Mobile software sports a cutting-edge wireless service, allowing you to search for scores, player stats, and schedules for the NBA, MLB, NHL, and PGA. NFL schedules should be coming soon, so by the time this book is published, they might be available. Did we mention that you can check for your flight status for arrival and departure as well? Or check for movie times and schedules and lots more information. And the best thing is, it's free. Download 4INFO at

www.blackberryfordummies.com/pearl/ten/four.html

Index

Notes

Notes

Notes

Notes

Notes

Notes

SPORTS, FITNESS, PARENTING, RELIGION & SPIRITUALITY

0-471-76871-5   0-7645-7841-3

Also available:
- Catholicism For Dummies 0-7645-5391-7
- Exercise Balls For Dummies 0-7645-5623-1
- Fitness For Dummies 0-7645-7851-0
- Football For Dummies 0-7645-3936-1
- Judaism For Dummies 0-7645-5299-6
- Potty Training For Dummies 0-7645-5417-4

- Buddhism For Dummies 0-7645-5359-3
- Pregnancy For Dummies 0-7645-4483-7 †
- Ten Minute Tone-Ups For Dummies 0-7645-7207-5
- NASCAR For Dummies 0-7645-768
- Religion For Dummies 0-7645-526
- Soccer For Dummies 0-7645-5229
- Women in the Bible For Dummies 0-7645-8475-8

TRAVEL

0-7645-7749-2   0-7645-6945-7

Also available:
- Alaska For Dummies 0-7645-7746-8
- Cruise Vacations For Dummies 0-7645-6941-4
- England For Dummies 0-7645-4276-1
- Europe For Dummies 0-7645-7529-5
- Germany For Dummies 0-7645-7823-5
- Hawaii For Dummies 0-7645-7402-7

- Italy For Dummies 0-7645-7386-1
- Las Vegas For Dummies 0-7645-7382-9
- London For Dummies 0-7645-427
- Paris For Dummies 0-7645-7630-5
- RV Vacations For Dummies 0-7645-4442-X
- Walt Disney World & Orlando For Dummies 0-7645-9660-8

GRAPHICS, DESIGN & WEB DEVELOPMENT

0-7645-8815-X   0-7645-9571-7

Also available:
- 3D Game Animation For Dummies 0-7645-8789-7
- AutoCAD 2006 For Dummies 0-7645-8925-3
- Building a Web Site For Dummies 0-7645-7144-3
- Creating Web Pages For Dummies 0-470-08030-2
- Creating Web Pages All-in-One Desk Reference For Dummies 0-7645-4345-8
- Dreamweaver 8 For Dummies 0-7645-9649-7

- InDesign CS2 For Dummies 0-7645-9572-5
- Macromedia Flash 8 For Dummies 0-7645-9691-8
- Photoshop CS2 and Digital Photography For Dummies 0-7645-9580-6
- Photoshop Elements 4 For Dumm 0-471-77483-9
- Syndicating Web Sites with RSS Fe For Dummies 0-7645-8848-6
- Yahoo! SiteBuilder For Dummies 0-7645-9800-7

NETWORKING, SECURITY, PROGRAMMING & DATABASES

0-7645-7728-X   0-471-74940-0

Also available:
- Access 2007 For Dummies 0-470-04612-0
- ASP.NET 2 For Dummies 0-7645-7907-X
- C# 2005 For Dummies 0-7645-9704-3
- Hacking For Dummies 0-470-05235-X
- Hacking Wireless Networks For Dummies 0-7645-9730-2
- Java For Dummies 0-470-08716-1

- Microsoft SQL Server 2005 For Dummies 0-7645-7755-7
- Networking All-in-One Desk Reference For Dummies 0-7645-9939-9
- Preventing Identity Theft For Dumr 0-7645-7336-5
- Telecom For Dummies 0-471-77085-X
- Visual Studio 2005 All-in-One Des Reference For Dummies 0-7645-9775-2
- XML For Dummies 0-7645-8845-1

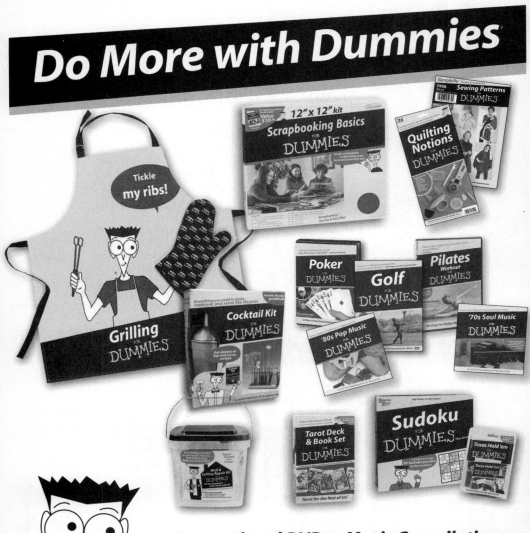